S0-AJL-399

SURVIVING AND PROSPERING IN THE MANAGED MENTAL HEALTH CARE MARKETPLACE

Tracy Todd
Brief Therapy Institute of Denver, Inc.

Practice Management Series
Series Editor: Bruce D. Forman

Professional Resource Press
Sarasota, Florida

Published by
Professional Resource Press
(An imprint of Professional Resource Exchange, Inc.)
Post Office Box 15560
Sarasota, FL   34277-1560

Printed in the United States of America

Copyright © 1994
by Professional Resource Exchange, Inc.

All rights reserved

No part of this book may be reproduced, stored in a retrieval system, or transmitted, in any form or by any means, either electronic, mechanical, photocopying, microfilming, recording, or otherwise, without written permission from the publisher.

The copy editor for this book was Patricia Hammond, the managing editor was Debra Fink, the production coordinator was Laurie Girsch, and the cover was created by Jami's Graphic Design.

Library of Congress Cataloging-in-Publication Data

Todd, Tracy. date.
    Surviving and prospering in the managed mental health care marketplace
/ Tracey Todd.
        p. cm. -- (Practice management series)
    Includes bibliographical references and index.
    ISBN 1-56887-004-3
    1. Managed mental health care--United States. I. Title.
II. Series: Practice management series (Sarasota, Fla.)
    [DNLM: 1. Mental Health Services--organization & administration-
-United States. 2. Managed Care Programs--organization &
administration--United States.   WM 30 1994]
RC465.6.T63   1994
362.2'0425'0973--dc20
DNLM/DLC
for Library of Congress   94-17985
                                                                  CIP

Acknowledgements

I would like to thank the partners at Employee Assistance Programs, Inc. - Jodie Collins, Lauren Behmer, Kathleen Steven, and Rick Polster - for allowing me to be part of an organization that is continuously trying to creatively contain mental health costs while maintaining exceptional clinical integrity. I am especially thankful to Jodie Collins for allowing me to stretch my creative energies and skills and for being an exceptional mentor to me.

I am thankful to Bruce D. Forman for offering me the opportunity to share my knowledge about this subject matter.

To Ted, Wilma, and Kim, I offer thanks for their perpetual support and understanding when it was most needed, and for being an exceptional family to be part of. Finally, I would like to thank Mark for being the best friend one could ask for, and for his continuous encouragement and support in all my endeavors.

Preface to the Series

News of so-called "health care reform" is reported by the media on a daily basis, and legislative proposals that will dramatically change the ways in which Americans receive and pay for health care are actively being discussed by politicians in both our state capitols and Washington. Although it is not clear at this time how mental health services will be incorporated into the reformed health care system, there likely will be dramatic changes in the philosophy of mental health treatment, authorization and reimbursement procedures, reporting and recordkeeping requirements, training expectations, and tracking of treatment outcomes and service utilization.

In order to survive and prosper in this new environment, mental health care providers must understand the implications of the reform movement for their practices and must develop strategies for coping with these changes. Although health care reform legislation is already creating practice-threatening crises for many practitioners, it is also creating a myriad of new opportunities for those who understand what is happening and who have developed skills for capitalizing on the newly emerging opportunities.

Titles in the *Practice Management Series* will address these practitioner needs as well as other issues that emerge with the continuing evolution of the practice environment. They are all designed to provide important new information and techniques for enhancing the business and professional development aspects of your practice and helping you adapt to the changes in health care delivery systems and procedures.

Although the focus and content of each book in this series is quite different, there are notable similarities:

1. Each title addresses a timely topic of critical importance for psychologists, clinical social workers, marriage and family therapists, psychiatrists, and other mental health practitioners who are trying to understand and develop survival skills for coping in the changing mental health marketplace.

2. All of the authors of books in this series were chosen for their ability to provide concrete "how-to-do-it" guidance to colleagues who are trying to gain new knowledge and expertise in dealing with complex practice management and professional development issues. Each title will include references and descriptions of available resources for maximizing benefits and helping readers gain increased knowledge on the discussed topics.

We feel that one of the unique assets of Professional Resource Press is the fact that all of its editorial decisions are made by mental health professionals. The publisher, series editors, and editorial reviewers are practicing psychologists, marriage and family therapists, clinical social workers, and psychiatrists.

If there are other topics you would like to see addressed in this series, please let us know.

Bruce D. Forman, PhD, Series Editor
Lawrence G. Ritt, PhD, Publisher

Table of Contents

SURVIVING AND PROSPERING IN THE MANAGED MENTAL HEALTH CARE MARKETPLACE

Chapter 1

Introduction

Psychotherapists have long been hoping that managed mental health care (MMHC) would simply go away. However, in recent years, it has become apparent that managed care is a process that is here to stay, and clinicians are going to have to learn to work with it.

The development of MMHC is partially due to the societal acceptance of mental health treatment. As the negative stereotypes about psychotherapy faded and individuals became less skeptical about filing insurance for psychotherapy, more individuals utilized mental health services. This increase in usage was soon felt by insurance companies that covered mental health services.

Insurance companies particularly felt the financial stress regarding the use of inpatient psychiatric settings. Kunnes (1992) reported that typically the design of the insurance plan was to favor inpatient care over outpatient care. Inpatient care is often covered at 90% while outpatient care is covered at 50%; it was common for inpatient hospitals to waive the copayment (Bacon, 1991). With this design package it was favorable for those who could not afford outpatient services to utilize an inpatient facility so their cost would be negligible. Other factors that contributed to higher utilization of mental health benefits included expansion of benefits, inpatient chains, incentives for psychiatrists to hospitalize, state-mandated benefits, deregulation and excess provider capacity, and unmet need (Bacon, 1991; Kunnes, 1992).

The result of this increased utilization of mental health services was increased costs to insurance companies, businesses, and
individuals. Businesses watched their costs of purchasing insurance plans increase dramatically, and employees continued to feel
the impact on their contribution to the plan. Managed care systems evolved as a way to check these increasing costs.

Managed care systems were designed to help contain the costs
of mental health and substance abuse service delivery by holding
treatment providers - both inpatient and outpatient - accountable
for the services delivered.   One of the roles of managed care
systems is to insure that monies allocated for mental health benefits* are being used in an efficient and effective manner. For the
first time, mental health professionals are being held accountable
for their services. Kunnes (1992) reported that one form of therapy used by psychiatrists is known as "wave therapy," that is,
wave to a patient, say "Hi," then bill for a full session. Managed
care systems demand that every session has a purpose and objective, and mental health professionals will need to learn to justify
their service delivery.

Another major change in service delivery is that psychotherapy
cannot constitute a process whereby a client merely "feels good."
Phrases such as "medically necessary" and "impact of life functioning" now are used to justify reimbursable service delivery.
Managed care systems require that clinicians explain and demonstrate that their methods are being effective and are needed. Mental health professionals often take exception to a third party informing them that the service they are delivering is not effective
enough or that it does not qualify for reimbursement. Psychotherapists have also been lured into believing that all mental and
behavioral health issues warrant payment by an insurer, and that
they should "be there" for their client in times of need - regardless
of the severity of the "need."

The introduction of MMHC is forcing treatment providers to
make many changes in their clinical and business styles. From a
clinical perspective, psychotherapists need to become more comfortable providing brief, symptom-relieving, problem-focused therapy. Additionally, some therapists will need to change the language they use in dialoguing about cases, becoming more be-

---

*For our purposes, the term mental health services will include substance abuse treatment.

havioral in the description of their cases. No longer can a clinician simply state that a client needs help improving self-esteem. Clinicians need to be concise as to what an improved self-esteem will "look like," how they are going to help the client achieve the goal, and what the termination criteria are. Many clinicians will have to brush the dust off a book on behaviorism they read in graduate school and begin to define problems in terms of frequency, rate, and duration. Clearly, behaviorists will have little adjustment to make regarding clinical language and process, while psychodynamic therapists will be challenged to change their language.

From a business perspective, treatment providers (even large hospital chains) must become aggressive in identifying managed care systems and gaining entry into the managed care networks. Treatment providers cannot rely on their faithful referral sources any longer. Although these sources can still make the well-intended referral, if the treatment provider is not in a particular network, the potential client will need to find another provider.

Regardless of one's opinion about managed care systems, they are here to stay. Coile (1992) reported numerous trends indicating that managed care is going to be the *modus operandi* for the 1990s. Some of these trends include indemnity plans converting to Preferred Provider Organization (PPO) and Health Maintenance Organization (HMO) designs, point of service designs increasing, and established HMOs and PPOs showing continued growth. Although managed care systems are going to dominate mental health benefit designs, these systems are still in their infancy and many challenges await them. In the meantime, treatment providers have their own challenges and adjustments to make in order to remain in business.

The purpose here will be to help clarify how managed care systems operate so that treatment providers can adjust to the current market. Additionally, strategies will be offered to help clinicians succeed in a managed care system. Although it will probably be a number of years before psychotherapists perceive managed care as an ally, they will need to make adjustments quickly in order to survive in a more competitive and challenging marketplace.

Chapter 2

Managed Care Systems

Managed competition is currently being used by the Clinton administration to describe its ideas about how to make health care available to more of the general population. The principle behind managed competition is to combine private free market structures with government regulation. Insurance agencies, managed care companies, and employers would be pooled to create large purchasing entities that would then contract with provider groups (e.g., PPOs, Exclusive Provider Organizations [EPOs], provider agencies). The managed care and insurance companies would compete for the business based of fees, quality of services, and effectiveness. Through government subsidies and taxes, such a plan would allow those without insurance coverage to have access to services. Additionally, managed competition would allow options for individual employers and subscribers to access multiple benefit packages.

It is believed that containing the cost of quality service delivery will not in and of itself create a successful competition system (Raso, 1993). Many other measures must be implemented and controlled for managed competition to have a chance of success. These measures include negotiated rates that limit fees, outcome research, use of preventive care, and decreasing administrative/bureaucratic costs (Raso, 1993).

Another important aspect of successful managed competition will be legal reformation. The current administration has consistently stated that this change is vital to the success of making health care available to the population. Astronomical legal fees and court settlements increase the cost of all professional services.

It is important to understand the impact of a managed competition system. Regardless of the design created by the Clinton administration, mental health providers at all levels (e.g., private practice, free-standing psychiatric hospitals) will be subject to management of their psychotherapy practices, and will be competing with other mental health professionals. The management component will consist of intrusiveness, accountability, and demonstrated effectiveness of service delivery. The competitive component will force mental health professionals to follow their clients and collect clinical information from them well after termination of therapy.

A common theme to any managed competition plan is cost-effective services. All health professionals, including mental health professionals, will be required to demonstrate quality services in a cost-effective manner. Individual practitioners and agencies will need to produce outcome data in order to be considered as a referral. No longer will simple satisfaction surveys be viewed as credible in determining therapeutic benefit. Every managed care company has experienced clients who were very happy with the services being offered by a psychotherapist, yet the problem that originated therapy remained. We will need to become more oriented toward effective and efficient therapy outcomes, and be able to measure and report these outcomes. Mental health professionals will need to tolerate a high level of accountability for their psychotherapy style. If managed competition is successful, the ultimate benefactor should be our clients.

Regardless of the design, managed care versus managed competition, insurance companies and employers need to make sure their mental health dollars are well spent. The concept of insuring well-spent dollars is not new to business, but it is new to mental health. For years, insurance companies have had a "hands-off," *carte blanche* attitude toward reimbursement of psychotherapy services. The result has been that psychotherapists have not had to account for themselves or compete for services based on outcome data. Mental health has now evolved into a corporate business, and we can either hide in our offices or begin to conceptualize our practices and operate as a business.

Every managed care system has unique characteristics and methods of operation. However, there are some core characteristics that differentiate these systems. These qualities and some important definitions and concepts will be outlined.

DEFINITIONS AND CONCEPTS

PREFERRED PROVIDER ORGANIZATION (PPO)

A PPO is a group of providers selected by a network model managed care system; these providers agree to deliver services for a reduced fee in hopes of a steady referral source. Their fees can be either set by the system or negotiated between the clinician and the managed care system. Additionally, providers will be requested to sign a contract that outlines the process and procedures they will follow after receiving a referral and what the agreed rate for services will be. The managed care system hopes to save money by having network providers who provide services at a discounted rate *and* provide therapy in a timely manner (brief therapy). The PPO is a benefit designed for the subscribers that provides incentive for its usage. Typically, the plan will have a reduced copayment and deductible for the subscriber if a provider from the PPO is used. The PPO is one plan in the benefit design, and it is the hope of the employer and the insurer that the incentive is great enough to lure a higher utilization over other plan options that are more costly. For example, a PPO plan in which the deductible is $50 for outpatient sessions with a copayment of $10 per session may be compared with an indemnity plan with a deductible of $250 and a copayment of 30% of total charge per session.

EXCLUSIVE PROVIDER ORGANIZATION (EPO)

An EPO is a group of providers contracted by the network model managed care system. Typically, two differences exist between the PPO and EPO: size and financial incentives. The EPO usually is smaller in size when compared to the PPO system. This allows more control by the network model managed care system regarding the service delivery of providers. The financial incentive with the EPO is that there is no choice of service plans. With an EPO, subscribers can receive services outside the organization only if they are willing to pay 100% of the costs; no other benefit options exist. While the subscriber may be limited in choices of psychotherapists and number of sessions per year, they may have a $50 deductible and a copayment of $5 per session. The EPO is designed to offer a greater financial incentive for the subscriber than the PPO but places a greater limitation on choices.

PROVIDER PROFILING

Provider profiling is an activity that managed care companies engage in to monitor a therapist's performance. This process can be as informal as making notes in a provider's file, or it can be as complex as a computer database system in which many variables are measured and recorded. Typically, the variables that a managed care system will be examining are costs per treatment episode, client satisfaction, client complaints, the results of a records review, administrative performance, clinical effectiveness, and cooperativeness with the managed care system. These variables help the managed care system make decisions about referral patterns and, potentially, which contracts, if any, may not be renegotiated after they expire.

PROSPECTIVE REVIEW

The prospective review is a process whereby the managed care system reviews documentation by a provider prior to service delivery in nonemergency situations. The treatment plan is reviewed by either a person in charge of authorizing care or a panel of individuals. The outcome of the review process is that the provider is given a set number of authorized sessions (outpatient) or days (inpatient) before another review is needed.

CONCURRENT REVIEW

Concurrent reviews are conducted during the course of treatment. The provider supplies the managed care system with documentation justifying why further treatment should be authorized. The concurrent review process is the most common process used in managed care. It is generally through this process that managed care systems learn which providers in their network warrant future inclusion and which do not. Due to the importance of completing a concurrent review, examples of weak and strong concurrent reviews will be presented later in this book.

RETROSPECTIVE REVIEW

Retrospective reviews are conducted following treatment. These reviews are rarely used because they are ineffective in managing benefits. A managed care system may conduct a retrospective review in costly and complicated cases in an attempt to determine if a more effective form of treatment could have been delivered.

CASE MANAGEMENT

Case management is an ongoing review of treatment. It is usually conducted for inpatient, partial care, structured outpatient, and complex outpatient cases. Case managers typically try to insure that these cases receive quality care without excessive or unnecessary treatment options (tests, added hospital days, etc.). An example of an often unnecessary treatment procedure is mandatory psychological testing upon admission to a hospital. Although such information can be interesting, it frequently does little to alter the treatment plan. Unless justification can be given for how the testing may alter the treatment plan, it most likely will be denied authorization for payment.

CARVE-OUT

In this benefit design, certain benefits are separated ("carved-out") from the total insurance package. For example, mental health benefits are carved-out of a total insurance package and then managed by another entity (managed care system). The idea of carving-out benefits is to create a distinct design that can be more efficiently and effectively managed.

CAPITATION

Capitation describes an arrangement in which a set fee is paid for service delivery. An example would be a private practice clinician agreeing to a set fee for reimbursement of $800 per referral. No matter how many sessions are used for treatment, the clinician will earn $800.

CAPITATED "AT RISK" BENEFIT PLAN

A capitated "at risk" benefit plan is designed so that a predetermined amount of money is earmarked for mental health services for a targeted amount of time (e.g., 1 year). A managed care system is then hired and directed to manage this money so that it lasts the duration of time determined. Often incentives are attached to such plans for the managed care system. For example, any money remaining from the allocated sum at the end of the year is turned over to the managed care system as profit. This type of design operates with some great financial risks because the managed care system will be responsible for any additional monies needed if the dollar amount granted by the employer and/or insurer is exceeded. For example, if after 11 months the allocated money has been exhausted, the managed care system will need to cover the costs of the remaining month. Prior to the contracting of the managed care system, the employer and insurer will need to be certain the managed care system is financially strong in the event of exhausting benefits. The outcome of exhausting the mental health benefits too soon will result in the managed care system not being rehired after the termination date of the contract. Furthermore, both the managed care system and the employer have their reputations at stake. Neither system wants to be perceived as placing money as a higher priority over the care the clients are receiving. Bacon (1991) cited that 68% of the companies surveyed reported their main concern as creating a balance between cost and quality of care. Companies are concerned that cost-cutting means a decrease in quality services (Bacon, 1991), and they do not want to be perceived by their employees as compromising their care.

ADMINISTRATIVE FEES PLAN

The administrative fees plan is a negotiated fee for managing the benefits that are agreed upon by the insurance company or business with the managed care system. Seldom are there incentives attached specifically to the monies available for mental health services. Typically, a business or insurance company will hire the managed care system, which is given a targeted percentage or dollar amount. For example, a business may have as a goal for the managed care system to keep the mental health costs from rising over 12% above the previous year's costs, and has agreed upon a set fee to pay the managed care system to accomplish this task, independent of the monies earmarked for mental health services. Although the managed care system has a financial responsibility to contain costs, its fee is not contingent upon the actual mental health dollars; it is paid an agreed-upon fee regardless of how well cost is contained. Also, no risks exist of exhausting the benefits prematurely.

TYPES OF SYSTEMS

POINT OF SERVICE

A point of service system is a benefit design whereby an employer offers different options for employees to choose from. An employer may have three different options available to employees for mental health benefits: a PPO, a staff model HMO (see below), and an indemnity plan. Each plan will have different financial requirements for usage, with financial incentives encouraging employees to use the staff model. The idea is to offer employees a choice of benefit designs while anticipating that employees will choose the design that is most financially advantageous for them.

STAFF MODEL MANAGED CARE SYSTEM

A staff model managed care system is a Health Maintenance Organization (HMO) in which treatment providers are typically employed as staff and paid a salary. The staff model provides most services and makes a referral only when special services, that cannot be provided by the organization, are needed. A staff model is used when monies need to be closely managed, as in a capitated at risk system.

GROUP MODEL MANAGED CARE SYSTEM

A group model managed care system is an HMO in which primary gatekeepers are identified (e.g., primary care physicians); these individuals make referrals to a contracted group to provide services at a capitated fee.

NETWORK MODEL MANAGED CARE SYSTEM

A network model managed care system is one in which providers are contracted by the managed care system to provide services at a discounted rate. Whether a PPO or EPO is utilized depends upon how aggressively the benefits will be managed. If a point of entry system is used by the employer, a PPO will be formed. However, if the employer chooses not to offer options to employees for mental health benefits, an EPO will be implemented.

HYBRID MODEL

A hybrid model is a combination of the staff and network models. The managed care system utilizing a hybrid model can take on many forms. For example, one managed care system using this model may have a one- to three-session staff model and then use a network for referring, while another system may have one to six sessions available prior to referring. The difference of only three sessions may seem insignificant, but the one- to six-session staff model allows the staff to do more than simply assess and refer. Frequently, six sessions are enough to provide assistance without a referral, and the managed care system saves money because network providers are not used. If the managed care system has provided solid training in brief therapy to its therapists, then they can deliver cost-effective and clinically efficient services. Increasingly, this type of mental health benefit design is being forged between managed care companies and employee assistance programs (EAP). For example, a managed care system and an EAP may combine forces in bidding on a contract so that the EAP offers a one- to three-session outpatient model and uses the network model managed care system when needing to refer.

Many factors determine which managed care system is used by an insurance company or employer. However, it is important that treatment providers understand the managed care system they have contracted with so that they can be realistic in their referral expectations and be aware of the intrusiveness of the managed care system. To highlight the continuum of differences between systems, two hypothetical managed care companies will be described.

THE ABC MANAGED CARE COMPANY

The ABC Managed Care Company was asked by the GeeWhiz Widget Corporation to manage GeeWhiz's mental health benefits. GeeWhiz offered ABC Managed Care Company an administrative fee for its services and requested that ABC set a goal of keeping its mental health care costs from exceeding a 12% annual increase. ABC knew that mental health costs for GeeWhiz had increased an average of 14% annually for the last 3 years and that it was projected to increase 18% in 1993 over the 1992 actual costs. The financial statement for GeeWhiz mental health expenses follows:

GEEWHIZ MENTAL HEALTH COSTS

	1990	1991	1992	1993 (projected)
Inpatient	$180,000	$222,300	$245,967	$304,284
Outpatient	$120,000	$119,700	$150,753	$163,846
TOTAL	$300,000	$342,000	$396,720	$468,130
	(+12%)	(+14%)	(+16%)	(+18%)

ABC recognizes that it will need to be somewhat aggressive in how it manages the mental health benefits. ABC sells GeeWhiz a hybrid model in which a one- to six-session staff model is attached to a PPO (network model). Employees of GeeWhiz who utilize ABC for services receive their first one to six sessions at no charge; if a referral is made, their copayment is $10 per session with no deductible. They are eligible for 25 outpatient visits per year and have a 40-day maximum eligibility for inpatient services. Their inpatient deductible is a one-time charge of $100. Employees who choose not to use this benefit design are given a second option. This option has a 30% copayment of total session charge for outpatient services with a deductible of $250. The inpatient design includes a 10% copayment for all costs, a $200 deductible per admission, and a maximum of 28 inpatient days. This second option allows the employee to choose any provider or hospital desired.

GeeWhiz hopes the majority of employees will take advantage of the financial incentive to enroll in the benefit design that ABC manages. While the second option allows employees to have a maximum of choice in providers, this choice costs more for the employer and employee.

The ABC Managed Care Company faces two immediate priorities in the management of benefits: First, it will focus on the inpatient mental health benefits. Second, it will try to deliver a majority of services through the use of its own staff and to decrease the number of referrals to private practice clinicians.

The first step for ABC is to negotiate pricing for inpatient services with select hospitals. For example, if a hospital usually charges $600 per day for inpatient services, ABC will try to negotiate a lower rate. The hospital hopes that the lower rate will increase the referrals from ABC. ABC will also implement a utilization review process whereby services are authorized in increments of 4 days.

How do these steps affect treatment providers? The hospital is affected by its need to become accountable for inpatient service delivery. It cannot simply warehouse patients, have psychiatrists practice "wave therapy," or have patients involved in a type of therapy that serves the hospital's needs instead of the patients'. Hospitals are also affected in that they can no longer assume they have a set number of days to treat the patient. Without the ABC Managed Care Company, the patient may have had a limit of 30 inpatient days per year around which the hospital could create a treatment plan. With ABC managing the benefits, the hospital needs to become efficient in treatment because the number of authorized inpatient days is determined by ABC. The hospital is also affected financially. ABC may have been able to negotiate a deal with the hospital for $480 per day instead of $600. Although the difference of $120 may seem insignificant for one day's services, it becomes very significant when many managed care programs are negotiating similar deals with the hospital. The rate reduction for hospital days forces the hospital system to become invested in providing a quality service that ABC finds satisfactory in hopes that ABC will send them more referrals.

For the private practice clinician who handles a proportion of inpatient service delivery, the inclusion of ABC in the treatment of the patient has a significant impact. The clinician can no longer count on three meetings a week with the patient for up to 4 weeks. Furthermore, psychotherapists will not be able to rely on hospitalization for treatment in the majority of cases, but rather will aim for stabilization and discharge. Clinicians will need to adjust to this shortened length of stay both financially and clinically.

ABC's second priority is to deliver efficient and effective outpatient services. Therapists at ABC will be expected to keep their referral rate lower than companies who use a one- to three-session model and to provide quality therapy services in one to six sessions. Therapists at ABC will be salaried, so their hourly rate for provision of services ($10+ per hour) will be less than that of network providers ($40 to $110 per hour). The ABC therapists will be trained in providing focused, problem-solving therapy so that the service delivery can be brief, meeting both ABC's and the client's needs.

ABC's provision of quality brief therapy affects the network provider in a number of ways. First, if a provider had a "connection" with someone in the GeeWhiz company prior to ABC's management of benefits, and received referrals from that person, ABC will most likely decrease these referrals. ABC will provide many of the services and determine which providers will be offered as choices to the client for a referral. Second, network providers who saw very few clients from the GeeWhiz company may see an increase in their caseload if they have a specialization needed by ABC. For example, ABC has many clients from GeeWhiz who present issues related to anxiety attacks. A PPO provider who specializes in Generalized Anxiety Disorder will most likely see an increase in referrals from ABC of employees from GeeWhiz.

A second area affecting network providers will be the intrusiveness of ABC. The ABC Managed Care Company staff may contact providers and ask if they would like a referral; they may inform the providers that sessions will be authorized only for a certain problem. For example, suppose an employee comes to ABC and presents the problem of having anxiety attacks. The ABC therapist discovers in the interview process that the client has experienced an increase in absenteeism and no longer participates in team functions within the workplace (e.g., committees). The ABC therapist feels that one to six sessions is not enough time to work on this issue and refers the client to its provider specialist on Generalized Anxiety Disorder. The ABC therapist may grant the provider 12 sessions, with the termination criteria being improved attendance and increased participation in committees (medically necessary). Unless new significant information becomes available that would lengthen treatment, the provider will be expected to complete treatment within the 12 sessions. If the provider is unable to complete the treatment, a concurrent review will need to be submitted requesting authorization for additional sessions.

Although the provider may discover during the therapy process that the client is also having difficulty with an aging parent (e.g., developing Alzheimer's), unless clear documentation can be given as to how that issue is impacting a major life function, sessions will not be authorized to deal with that issue. The provider will need to keep focused on dealing with the absenteeism and participation in committees. This focus is often difficult for providers who have had a history of being free to treat any and all issues presented by their clients.

The impact on the provider is clear. The provider needs to adjust to having someone else suggest what the treatment plan should be, and the provider is now accountable for the effectiveness of the therapy sessions. If the provider finds that 12 sessions are not enough, the concurrent review process begins.

The intrusiveness of the ABC Company manifests in another way. ABC will want to know what is happening in therapy - particularly if 12 sessions were not enough to accomplish treatment goals - and when therapy will be concluded. If, referring to the previous example, the provider decides to work on the issue of the parent with Alzheimer's, solid documentation will be needed to justify the treatment, demonstrate medical necessity, and outline a clear strategy for how the treatment will improve the employee's attendance and participation.

At the completion of the contract year between the GeeWhiz Widget Corporation and the ABC Managed Care Company, the financial statement will be examined. If the financial statement demonstrates cost-containment, ABC will most likely be rehired to manage the benefits for another contract term. If, however, ABC was unable to contain costs, it will most likely be replaced by another managed care system. The following financial statement would warrant the managed care system being rehired:

GEEWHIZ MENTAL HEALTH COSTS

	1990	1991	1992	1993 (actual)
Inpatient	$180,000	$222,300	$245,967	$254,397
Outpatient	$120,000	$119,700	$150,753	$191,913
TOTAL	$300,000	$342,000	$396,720	$446,310
	(+12%)	(+14%)	(+16%)	(+12.5%)

The ABC Managed Care Company described here is a skeletal description of a network model managed care system, utilizing a

PPO and operating out of an administrative-fee-only system. Many variations of this model exist, and it is important for the provider working with a managed care system to become familiar with the unique characteristics of the system he or she contracts with. One distinguishing characteristic is the number of sessions allowed by a clinician within the managed care system before referring. The greater the number of sessions, the fewer referrals.

XYZ HEALTH SYSTEMS

XYZ Health Systems was hired by the WE CARE Insurance Company to manage its mental health benefits. WE CARE Insurance agreed to a 1-year contract with XYZ Health Systems for an allocated sum of money earmarked for mental health benefits. One business that subscribes to WE CARE Insurance is Wicky-Wack Gadgets. WickyWack Gadgets had the following financial statement when WE CARE was hired to manage the mental health benefits:

WICKYWACK GADGETS
MENTAL HEALTH CARE COSTS

	1990	1991	1992	1993 (projected)
Inpatient	$236,250	$262,725	$309,168	$341,824
Outpatient	$138,750	$161,025	$173,907	$218,543
TOTAL	$375,000	$423,750	$483,075	$560,367
	(+11%)	(+13%)	(+14%)	(+16%)

XYZ Health Systems agreed to a contract with WE CARE Insurance Company that the allocated sum of money earmarked for mental health benefits will be $550,000 annually; XYZ Health Systems will be at risk if the benefits exceed $550,000. If XYZ is able to keep the mental health costs under $550,000, the balance will be retained as its fee for managing the benefits (profit). Also, WE CARE will keep its benefit payments to an acceptable level, and WickyWack will be able to keep its contribution to the benefit plan manageable. Finally, the employees of WickyWack will not experience a significant increase in their contribution to the plan design.

Through the XYZ Health Systems, the employees of Wicky-Wack Gadgets now have a benefit design in which they are eligible for a maximum of 20 outpatient visits per year and 45 inpatient days per year. They must use only the XYZ Health Systems for services or assume responsibility for 100% of payments. They have a $50 outpatient deductible and no copayment for outpatient services. Inpatient services have a $100 deductible and a copayment of $50 per admission.

What are the priorities of the XYZ Health Systems? XYZ has a lot at stake in this agreement. Not only must it provide quality services, but it needs to manage the benefits aggressively so it does not exhaust the $550,000. If it fails to keep the costs under $550,000, it not only loses its fee for providing the service, but at the end of the contracted time period it will most likely lose the contract with WE CARE. So a primary priority is to save money.

The first priority of XYZ will be to cut inpatient costs. Similar to the PPO design, hospitals will need to settle for a decrease in pricing for inpatient days. Additionally, fewer hospitals will be recruited to be part of the EPO, and those that are utilized will be expected to stabilize and discharge the patient as quickly as possible. This situation puts the hospital and XYZ at some risk. The hospital will want to maintain the business of XYZ, so they will try to discharge a patient quickly - possibly too quickly. Unlike the ABC Managed Care Company, XYZ Health Systems may authorize treatment in increments of 1, 2, or 3 days. Most likely, someone from XYZ will be reviewing the case and patient on a daily basis to insure that hospitalization is warranted.

The effect on the private practice clinician is substantial. First, there will be very few referrals made by the XYZ Health Systems clinicians. It will be the philosophy of XYZ Health Systems to provide all outpatient treatment through its own clinicians. Providers who once saw a good referral source from say, an internal EAP, will now experience a rare referral by XYZ Health Systems. Second, getting into the EPO used by the XYZ Health Systems will be a difficult process. The XYZ Health Systems is going to be certain the network providers are knowledgeable in brief therapy, and it is possible that network providers will be expected to attend trainings held by XYZ so that they are theoretically and clinically forming a cooperative relationship. Another area to be impacted will be the number of sessions authorized by XYZ Health Systems. The number of sessions authorized prior to a concurrent review being needed may be three sessions. The more concurrent reviews requested, the more influence XYZ has in treatment goals and termination criteria.

At the end of the year, XYZ Health Systems was able to produce the following financial statement:

WICKYWACK GADGETS
MENTAL HEALTH CARE COSTS

	1990	1991	1992	1993 (actual)
Inpatient	$236,250	$262,725	$309,168	$281,343
Outpatient	$138,750	$161,025	$173,907	$259,701
TOTAL	$375,000	$423,750	$483,075	$541,044
	(+11%)	(+13%)	(+14%)	(+12%)

The earmarked sum of money was $550,000, so XYZ Health Systems made a profit of $8,956. Now XYZ Health Systems and the WE CARE Insurance Company must decide whether they will work with each other for another year. WE CARE Insurance Company will factor in any complaints they had from WickyWack Gadgets' employees about their usage of XYZ Health Systems. If there were many complaints about the system, WE CARE Insurance Company will not want to jeopardize its status as Wicky-Wack's carrier and may not extend a new contract to XYZ Health Systems. Similarly, XYZ Health Systems will assess its confidence about the potential profitability of managing the benefits for the WE CARE Insurance Company regarding WickyWack Gadgets. If it does not feel the capitated dollar amount set by WE CARE Insurance Company or WickyWack Gadgets is realistic enough to be profitable, it may not elect to be the managed care system for WE CARE Insurance Company.

XYZ Health Systems as described here is but one example of a staff model managed care system, utilizing an EPO and operating a capitated at risk benefit design. Although this model appears to be intrusive and more concerned with financial factors than the ABC Managed Care Company, it has some advantages for the network provider and employees covered by the design package. As a network provider, if the clinician adheres to brief therapy principles and techniques and gets accepted to the EPO, working with XYZ should be no different from conducting therapy sessions with any other client. Additionally, because fewer providers are typically used, the referrals should help balance the intrusiveness of the system.

On the surface, it may appear that a system such as XYZ's is concerned primarily with finances. However, this type of system allows insurance companies to offer some kind of mental health benefits to businesses for their employees, even though the benefits may be negligible. With some creative planning, XYZ Health Systems could provide a quality, innovative service and be profitable. States that mandate specific minimal standards for outpatient visits and inpatient days in insurance designs for businesses are often requiring the business to make available services that it cannot afford to purchase. A plan such as XYZ's allows businesses to try to meet the state mandate.

Regardless of the type of managed care system being utilized, it must be remembered that the system is purchased by either an insurance company or an employer. With both systems, the objective is to contain the mental health costs. The difference between the two systems is that the capitated at risk system of XYZ Health Systems can often create a clouding of priorities. Even though they are trying to make clinically appropriate decisions, they have a greater financial awareness. Systems such as XYZ often create mechanisms to deal with clients who need immediate attention that are effective and cost-saving. One example is the use of crisis groups. These group meetings not only cut down on the individual hours needed for one-to-one meetings, but they also allow the clinician to assess who needs the most immediate attention. Although such innovations can be viewed distastefully and possibly have disastrous results, it is such innovations that will begin to keep rising mental health costs in check.

In both examples of managed care systems, network providers were utilized for service delivery. The most common questions usually asked by psychotherapists have to do with how to get into such networks and get referrals.

Chapter 4

Identifying
And Applying to
Provider Networks

IDENTIFYING MANAGED
CARE SYSTEMS

Identifying managed care systems can be a difficult process. Described here are some ways to learn what managed care organizations are in your area.

JOB POSTINGS

Look for job openings posted in any publication that has an employment section (e.g., newspaper). Frequently, when a managed care system is in the process of signing an agreement with a business or insurance company, it will advertise a job opening. These jobs may be listed under titles such as provider relations director, network coordinator, utilization review coordinator, or clinical director. The managed care system may need someone in the area to coordinate the development of a local provider network and hire the necessary employees to manage the benefit package. Writing for more information about the job will give you the name of the company and possibly a contact person. You should not rely on their contacting you when the position is filled, but rather keep inquiring about how the process of building the network is progressing.

BUSINESS NEWS

The local business paper or business section of your paper can often give clues as to what is happening in the community regarding managed care systems. If a new business is relocating to your area, try to find out what its insurance policy is going to be. Conversely, you may discover that a business is laying off employees; if you have been trying to get into the system that manages that company's benefits, it may be wiser to investigate another system.

EMPLOYEE ASSISTANCE
PROFESSIONAL ASSOCIATION (EAPA)

The Employee Assistance Professional Association is an organization that meets on a regular basis and is an excellent forum for increasing knowledge and meeting with managed care professionals. The purpose of EAPA is to expose employee assistance professionals to a variety of treatment modalities and programs. There is a membership process, but typically a few visits will be allowed before you are asked to become a member. Take advantage of this opportunity to see if this is an organization you feel will benefit you professionally. The format of the meeting usually allows for plenty of networking among professionals. This networking can pay off in identifying any new systems in town that should be investigated. If you do not know when EAPA meets in your area, ask someone who works extensively with employee assistance programs or call the national EAPA office at (703) 522-6272.

NETWORKING WITH PROVIDERS
ALREADY IN CURRENT NETWORKS

Probably the single best way to identify managed care networks is to associate yourself with mental health professionals who work with managed care systems and are comfortable doing so. They may not have any leverage in assisting your acceptance to systems, but they certainly can provide for you names, addresses, and phone numbers of the key people within managed care systems. I recently had lunch with a friend who has a private practice and does a solid managed care business. After we got settled and ordered our lunch, our conversation focused on provider networks. We each listed the networks we were part of and exchanged information on whom to contact for those networks we were not part of.

Not only can these colleagues be helpful in identifying managed care systems, but they can also be valuable resources in helping you to work in a cooperative manner with managed care. Many excellent clinicians have great difficulty working in a cooperative manner with managed care. You want to network with those clinicians who are successful with managed care.

One method of networking is to identify 8 to 10 other mental health professionals, who are geographically diverse and have different areas of clinical interest, and begin meeting monthly. During these meetings it is important to share managed care information, marketing strategies, and administrative "secrets" that help providers become more efficient in paperwork and case management. Because this will be a diverse group, trust can be established quicker because you will not be competing with one another.

APPLYING TO A SYSTEM

Unless you know someone within the system who can get you an application and lobby for your inclusion in the system, you will need to convince someone within the managed care system that you should be given the opportunity to apply for their consideration. If you cannot arrange a personal meeting, you will have to use a letter to try to get an application sent to you. This letter should be short, and should focus on how you can help the managed care system meet its objectives. See Appendix A (p. 69) for an example of this type of letter.

Depending upon the system, the application can range from 2 to 15 pages. Try not to be intimidated by the application, and be complete when filling it out. Your application will need to convince the system that it should accept you. Simply receiving an application does not guarantee your acceptance. When applying to a managed care system, there are a number of issues you should be aware of and items you should emphasize.

PERFORMANCE BASED PRACTICE

One of the most attractive items you can enclose in an application is the process you use to measure your efficiency and effectiveness. Some areas to emphasize include the following: average number of sessions per diagnosis, client satisfaction ratings, range of presented problems dealt with, and percentage of cases that did not have any administrative errors during a calendar year (e.g., concurrent reviews submitted on time).

SPECIALTIES

It is usually advantageous to be very specific when identifying your specialties. For example, family therapy used to be a specialty. However, that category is now being filled by many therapists. A specialization within family therapy might be family therapy with families who recently experienced trauma (e.g., murder, robbery, accidental death). Although this specialization may not gain you many referrals, it may insure that you get any referrals with this population. Specialization can go on *ad infinitum*, but giving specifics can be beneficial. If you have any documentation of specialized training, be sure to include it with your application.

GENDER ISSUES

If you maintain a practice that emphasizes a particular gender or gender issue, be sure to document it on your application. Examples of such issues are men who have been sexually molested, women who have been raped, and men whose wives were victims of incest.

RELIGIOSITY

Provided you are comfortable marketing your religious leanings regarding psychotherapy, you should give this information to the managed care system. Quite often clients ask managed care systems if they can be referred to a "Christian counselor," or a counselor of some other religious orientation.

PUBLICATIONS AND PRESENTATIONS

It is imperative that you let the managed care system know you are a published provider, particularly if you have written a book or published in referenced journals. Presentations at state and national conferences should also be listed. Listing presentations for local organizations may be helpful, but these are less impressive to those who review your application. Publications and presentations not only give you a chance at being accepted into the organization, but they also have the potential to present you as the "expert" in a certain clinical area within the provider network.

YOU ARE NOT OMNIPOTENT

Although you may take pride in your abilities to work with any type of clientele, remember, you cannot work with every type of problem presented. Providers often feel that if they indicate that they can work with virtually any problem, they will have a better chance of being accepted and gaining referrals. Most applications restrict potential network providers to identifying a specific number of specialty areas. For example, the application may ask providers to indicate 5 areas out of a list of 20 that they feel comfortable working with. If, however, the managed care organization decides it wants to interview applicants or those who are already accepted, you are well advised to be able to identify specific populations or problem areas that you do *not* want to work with. Providers who present themselves as experts in all areas will be viewed with great suspicion and most likely used minimally by the managed care system if accepted to the network.

LICENSE AND DEGREE

Although you will undoubtedly be asked to identify your license and degree, be specific about your degree area. Managed care systems often establish a ratio of how many providers they want per license type and discipline. For example, a managed care system may want to have 100 clinical psychologists and 75 doctoral-level marital therapists. If you have a doctoral degree in the area of marriage and family therapy, you may get accepted into the network because the network had not yet reached its quota

of marriage and family therapists. However, if you had not ac-
knowledged what discipline your doctorate was in, you may not
have been accepted because the clinical psychologist quota had
been met.

CREDENTIALS

Most providers will indicate their educational degrees and
licenses, but it is always a good idea to list any other credentials
you may have. Remember, you do not know who has applied and
been accepted to the system. You may possess a certain credential
that is lacking in the network. Furthermore, you do not know the
corporate attitude of the managed care system, and a particular
credential may be just what is needed to gain acceptance. Include
any documentation as evidence of these credentials. Some credentials you should be certain to list follow:

- Certified Employee Assistance Professional
- Certified Alcohol Counselor (list levels if pertinent)
- Certified Hypnotherapist
- Clinical member of the American Association for Marriage
  and Family Therapy
- Board Diplomate of Social Work
- Fluency in a foreign language
- American Sign Language

GEOGRAPHIC LOCATION

Be sure to list any and all satellite offices you have access to
for providing mental health services. Even if you are subletting
an office for only a half day, be sure to document it on the application. The managed care system may lack a certain type of
provider in a certain area, and if you meet its need, you could be
accepted based on a location you use even minimally.

GROUP THERAPY

Group therapy is an excellent option for providing services for
managed mental health care systems. Such systems are continu-
ally trying to find quality group therapy practices. Group therapy

is not only cost-effective, but it is also a good clinical option for many clients.

A common mistake made by clinicians, when asked by managed care systems if they practice group therapy, is the response that they are willing to run a group, but they are unable to produce a start date or target population. It is amazing how many providers are "about to" start a group but cannot produce dates, times, or topics. If you feel comfortable running a group, be specific about it to the managed care system. Two suggestions may be helpful. First, develop a flyer advertising the group. Clinicians in the managed care system can copy it, discuss it with clients in their office, and, it is hoped, answer questions clients may ask. Second, run a time-limited group. A time-limited group demonstrates that you have a specific agenda for clients; the managed care system will not be as concerned as with a support group that goes on indefinitely.

SELL YOURSELF

The best way to approach the application process is as if you were applying for a job. Traditionally, mental health professionals have been hesitant to "toot their own horn," but when applying to a managed care system it is important to do so. Remember, if the system has been in existence for a period of time, your application is competing with other applicants and current providers. If an existing managed care system is accepting applications for network providers, it can mean that the network is lacking certain specialties or it is expanding in size to account for increased business. You need to demonstrate that you are worth accepting! With developing managed care systems, you do not know what other mental health professionals have applied to the network, so you need to make yourself stand out.

MANAGED CARE SENSITIVITY

Clearly communicate that you are knowledgeable and experienced with the clinical and financial objectives of managed care. Some of the following are selling points that demonstrate your ability to work with such systems:

- be a consultant for another managed care system
- supervise managed care and/or EAP clinicians
- conduct utilization reviews for a company
- train clinicians in brief therapy

Foos, Ottens, and Hill (1991) discussed how psychologists can use their research skills to quantitatively demonstrate their therapeutic effectiveness. You do not need to be a psychologist to conduct your own research, but Foos et al. (1991) stress how important it will be for such research to exist. The ability to document your understanding of how managed care systems operate and that you can cooperate with these systems will be invaluable on your application.

WARNING!

When applying to managed care systems, you will minimally be asked to complete two documents: an application and a contract. The contract is a legally binding document, and you may want to have an attorney review the contract if you do not feel comfortable signing the document. One clause that is frequently included in the contract resembles a "No Compete Clause." This clause may vary among managed care systems. The essence of a "No Compete Clause" is that you will not use the concepts, methods, or ideas of the managed care system to develop your own system, or you will not participate directly with other systems (e.g., consult). It is highly unlikely that you will be asked not to be involved with other managed care systems at the provider level, but it is common that you are required not to consult, supervise, or eventually develop your own network for whatever purposes.

Be sure you are comfortable signing such an agreement, because you never know what tomorrow will bring. Typically, such clauses will give a time period following the termination of your contract within which you are prohibited from engaging in such activities. These clauses can be tricky, especially if you have a positive reputation in working with managed care systems that may lead to your being asked to consult, advise, or sit on a committee.

Recently, I applied to two different managed care systems that had such clauses. In one case I asked the company to remove the clause, but it would not, so I did not sign the contract and become a network provider. In the other case, the company sent me a new contract with the clause deleted, so I signed it and became a member. It was my opinion that neither system would generate enough referrals to warrant my agreeing not to compete with them.

A second contractual area to be cautious of involves indemnification. Indemnification, essentially a "hold harmless" clause in a contract, attempts to protect managed care systems from lawsuits filed against a mental health professional. When you sign a contract with such a clause, you are generally saying, "I hold the managed care system harmless for any actions on my part." However, it is important that there be mutual indemnification. With mutual indemnification, the managed care system also holds you harmless for adverse consequences resulting from a wrongful act by the managed care system. I strongly encourage all providers to have this section reviewed by their attorney so that they are fully cognizant of the implications of signing contracts, with or without a mutual indemnification clause.

```
┌─────────────────────────────────────┐
│                                     │
│           Chapter 5                 │
│                                     │
│       Getting Referrals             │
│                                     │
│                                     │
└─────────────────────────────────────┘
```

After mental health professionals are accepted to a managed care system, they wonder why they do not receive immediate and abundant referrals. After you are accepted to a network, your name is added to a list of other providers; this list can frequently be in the hundreds. Even though you are accepted, you now need to differentiate yourself from other providers so you can maximize your potential to gain referrals. You have not yet been used by the system, so you will need to change their referral habits and gain their confidence that you will deliver efficient, quality service in a cost-effective manner. Where do you start?

IDENTIFY REFERRAL SOURCES

INDIVIDUAL CLINICIANS

It is imperative that individual clinicians within the managed care system know about you. These clinicians are the front line of the managed care system and are exposed to many different clients and presenting problems. In some systems, the role of these clinicians may be to assess, refer, and negotiate with the provider what is expected from treatment. These clinicians will be making many referrals, and you will want to be in their minds when the need comes up. In other systems, clinicians may be given up to 10 sessions to work with clients and will make relatively few referrals. When clinicians have the opportunity to provide services for a length of time, they may refer out only 25% of the cases. Even in managed care, the saying, "I don't refer to places, I refer to people" holds true. Try to arrange a meeting with clinicians from within the managed care system and be prepared to explain why you should receive the referrals. When meeting with the clinicians, plan on spending a maximum of 15 minutes unless you have prearranged a longer meeting or luncheon. These clinicians are bombarded by requests to meet with network providers, and they usually do not have a great deal of time to meet with you. Although meeting with individual clinicians is a positive maneuver to gain referrals, it can take a great deal of time, as many managed care systems employ a number of clinicians.

CLINICAL SUPERVISOR

Meeting with the clinical supervisor is often more advantageous and efficient than meeting with individual clinicians. Managed care systems usually utilize a group supervision or team meeting format to discuss cases and obtain referral sources from one another. Clinical supervisors can be pivotal in directing any referrals in these group meetings because they interface with all clinicians.

UTILIZATION REVIEWER

Clinical supervisors may perform utilization reviews, or specific individuals within the system could be given this role. Those who perform utilization review, both inpatient and outpatient, are knowledgeable of the network providers that follow the managed care philosophy and deliver quality services in an efficient manner. They have a clear understanding of what the network lacks from its providers and often look for someone new to give opportunities to. If they use you for a case, and you fit with what they expect, you may gain more referrals.

AUTHORIZER OF REFERRALS

Many managed care companies employ their own internal system for making referrals. If clinicians want to make a referral to a network provider, they may need to obtain authorization from someone within their system. The person who can give authorization may be the utilization reviewer, a supervisor, or someone else. It is especially important for you to meet this person. He or she has direct say about which network providers will be used and which ones will not. It is a good idea to always maintain a positive relationship with these individuals. You could be a great clinician, but if you were to alienate one of these people they may utilize another clinician with equal skills instead of you.

MEET WITH MEMBERS
OF THE SYSTEM

If you are fortunate enough to meet with someone within the system, make good use of your time. Inquire about how their system operates, the percentage of referrals they make to network providers, and how you could help them meet their clinical and financial objectives. Some information you will want to obtain from them regarding their system, if they will disclose it, is the percentage of referrals made, who authorizes the referrals, how many sessions they typically authorize on the initial referral, and what they expect from the provider (see Appendix B, p. 71, for sample questions). You should also ask if you could attend a staff meeting to introduce yourself to the group of clinicians within the managed care system. Have a clear understanding of how much time you have been given to introduce yourself and try not to overstay your welcome.

Another method of gaining referrals is by providing inservice training for clinicians of the managed care system. They, too, appreciate continuing education that will help them do their jobs better. You can use your knowledge and experience to educate them about your specialty, and they will hopefully perceive you as a quality clinician and their network "expert." They also associate a name with a face, and you establish yourself as a credible provider.

It is important that when you market yourself to a managed care system, you keep in mind its financial and clinical objectives. Most providers market themselves with the attitude of "I am a good therapist and I want your referrals." Seldom does a provider use the marketing strategy of "I understand your managed care obligations, and here is how I can help you meet them."

KEEP THE REFERRALS COMING

Your first referral may be the managed care system's test of your service delivery. There are a few things you need to do and be aware of.

Sometimes managed care systems will give you a summary sheet or checklist to follow during the therapy process. This checklist may include such items as the amount of the client's copayment, billing procedures for no-show appointments, preauthorization phone numbers, and how to bill for services. Frequently, providers do not clearly understand the process involved and, for example, do not submit their bill with the adequate forms and then do not get paid. When this occurs, the clinician becomes upset with the managed care system and vice versa; the result is that clients become anxious or involved in an issue that they should not be involved in. Administrative snags not only leave a bad impression for all parties involved but can also jeopardize your relationship with the system. A good partnership between a network provider and the managed care system should result in a relationship between the two that is imperceptible to the client (Penzer, 1990). If a managed care company does not provide a checklist about what steps need to be followed when accepting a referral, develop your own. This checklist will save you a great deal of time and frustration. See Appendix C (p. 73) for an example of what may be included on the checklist.

A second area of concern is providing quality care. It almost seems that this issue should not need to be addressed, yet there are cases in which providers either take a referral that they are not qualified for or do not solve the client's presenting problem. I consulted with a network provider who recently had accepted a referral of an adolescent for family therapy. During the treatment process, the provider began to see the adolescent individually and documented this treatment on a concurrent review. I inquired as to why the treatment focus shifted to individual therapy, and the provider communicated discomfort in working with the systemic tension. We agreed that the tension was needed to promote some positive changes in the family, and the provider gave family therapy another chance. To the provider's credit, the provider was willing to consult with me about the case and consider referring the family out if treatment goals could not be reached. Due to the clinician's receptiveness, I would not hesitate about making another referral to this clinician.

Another example of a provider jeopardizing the possibility of receiving additional referrals is when a referral was made to help a client deal with depression so that he could go back to work. Upon receiving the concurrent review (8 weeks later), the provider documented that the client continued to be absent a great deal of time from work and that the treatment focus was childhood issues. Although these issues may have been important for the therapy process, the referral was made with the understanding that the primary focus was to get the client back to work. If the provider does not get the employee back to work, the referring clinician in the managed care system will feel that the provider did not do the contracted job and may not send any more referrals.

A third area to keep in mind is how you are saving money for the managed care system by taking the referral. When you get a referral you will be compared to other network providers who get similar referrals in terms of length of treatment and client satisfaction. If your service delivery consistently takes considerably longer than other network providers, the managed care system may not make future referrals because you are not saving them money (economic credentialing). You probably will not know how long other providers are taking to provide a similar service, but the managed care system may provide hints and suggestions that you need to become more efficient in your use of sessions. These helpful hints usually come in the form of a letter or phone call inquiring about the treatment status of clients. A psychiatrist called me one afternoon to inquire about how he was doing compared to other network providers. I informed him that it appeared he never terminated with clients, and he stated he had terminated with all referrals he had received. Through our discussion, we discovered he was providing problem-focused therapy but was not sending in termination summaries on the clients. Not sending termination summaries gave the impression that this psychiatrist was not providing services that fit with managed care, and subsequently he had been discontinued as a referral source.

FIRST SESSION ESSENTIALS

There are a few tasks that need to be completed during the first session to help you get off to a good start with a referral from a new managed care company. First, get a release of information signed by the client that enables you to speak with the referral source. You will need to explain why you need to speak with a case manager or utilization reviewer, and obtaining the release will help you in case management and in crisis situations. Second, have your clients sign a claim form. On the claim form there are two important areas that need to be explained to clients. The assignment of benefits section allows you, as their provider, to be paid directly so that your clients do not need to pay your contracted rate. The release of medical information section should be explained to your clients so that they are aware the payor of benefits will be getting personal information such as diagnosis and style of therapy (e.g., family therapy). Finally, it is imperative that you explain to your clients how their managed care benefit design operates. Informing them about how many sessions have been initially authorized, how the utilization review system operates, and the concept of medically necessary services will help create a more positive team approach to treatment. Of primary importance is explaining these policies and procedures in a positive frame of reference so that the managed care is *not* perceived as a nemesis to clients or the therapist.

CONCURRENT REVIEW PROCESS

Another area that can make a difference in whether referrals will continue is the concurrent review process. This process is used when a provider needs to obtain authorization for more sessions to treat a client. Because this process is vitally important to a provider's survival, a case example will be used.

You were referred a client, Jeff,* who is 32 years old, experiencing single episode major depression, moderate. Jeff has been married 5 years and has a 2-year-old son. The depression is affecting his work attendance, but when at work he is able to perform satisfactorily. He misses about 2 days of work per week due to the depression. The marriage is solid, but there are some financial stressors resulting from his work absenteeism, and these stressors have created some conflict in the marriage. Jeff's mental health benefit package allows him a maximum of 25 outpatient visits per year. As a provider you were given 10 sessions to complete treatment. You have conducted eight sessions and feel additional sessions are needed to complete your treatment goals. In order to obtain approval for these sessions you will need to complete what is typically referred to as a concurrent review. See Appendix D (pp. 75-78) for examples of weak and strong concurrent reviews.

AREAS OF EMPHASIS
IN REVIEW PROCESS

Diagnosis. The strong concurrent review used all five axes and wrote out the primary diagnosis. The Global Assessment of Functioning (GAF) and Severity of Psychosocial Stressors ratings supported one another. The weaker review listed a single, incomplete number. Weaker reviews are usually vague in description; often the provider will list a series of primary diagnoses and not use remaining axes.

Assessment. The strong concurrent review documented more verifiable facts and placed less emphasis on a theory than the weaker review. The strong review also indicated that the provider has a therapeutic direction. The assessment set the stage for what seemed like a reasonable treatment plan. The assessment should be consistent with the remainder of the concurrent review and follow a logical flow.

Treatment Plan and Goals. The strong review indicated specific behavioral goals as compared to the theoretical goals of

---

*Names and identifying characteristics of persons in all case examples are fictitious.

the weaker review. These goals also fit with why Jeff was referred to the network provider (job attendance). Also, the treatment goals indicated that the therapist was giving Jeff responsibility for the treatment through the use of between-session tasks.
Weaker reviews tend to highlight what the therapist and client are
accomplishing in the session rather than between sessions.

Response to Treatment. The weaker concurrent review did
not give any indication of Jeff's current condition related to work,
marriage, or depression. The strong review listed precisely what
Jeff's response to treatment was and indicated the provider was
keeping in mind the reason for the referral (job attendance).

Termination Criteria. The strong concurrent review listed
the termination criteria and used job attendance as one criterion.
Furthermore, the goals of reduced symptoms and a minimum GAF
score of 75 are more realistic than the termination criterion of the
weaker review (understanding childhood experiences) which may
take considerable time to accomplish. The weaker review also
stated that no foreseeable termination date could be seen. There
are cases in which it is unlikely that clients will ever terminate,
but a managed care system usually identifies and discusses them
with the provider. In Jeff's example, termination was to occur
when he was going back to work, and there was no significant
information disclosed by the provider to argue that Jeff could not
have a projected termination date for therapy. The weaker review
communicated to the managed care system that the provider had
lost focus of why the referral was made.

Additional Sessions Needed. Although the weaker concurrent
review indicated 15 more sessions were needed to complete treatment, a reviewer would be very suspicious if the provider had any
immediate intent to terminate treatment. In the "Termination Criteria" section the provider noted that therapy may not end in the
foreseeable future. A reviewer may wonder how the provider
chose 15 as the number of sessions needed to complete treatment.
Providers often become upset with hospitals when hospitals develop treatment plans around the maximum number of days the
patient is eligible for treatment, but many providers do the same
thing when they discover the maximum number of outpatient visits
allowed for their client. The strong concurrent review outlined a

strategy for allowing therapy to proceed and terminate which was consistent with the entire review, and 12 sessions seemed realistic.

DISCUSSION

The difference between the strong concurrent review and the weak concurrent review is in specificity. The strong review documented what was specifically being addressed in therapy and did not overindulge in theory. The person who reads your concurrent review may not share your theoretical viewpoint of what is occurring or even be knowledgeable in that theory. It is imperative that your concurrent review is as behavioral as possible so that the reviewer can gain a good understanding of what is occurring in the therapy process.

Many providers will overcomplete the concurrent review form, perhaps feeling that the more they document, the better their chance of gaining the additional sessions requested. More does not equal better. In contrast, a strong review is often short and always very specific.

When requesting more sessions, make sure the number you request is consistent with the treatment described. As in the weaker concurrent review example, providers often ask for a number of sessions without justifying why they need that many. Frequently, the number they request is coincidentally the balance of the number of sessions that the client is eligible for per year. In Jeff's example, he was eligible for a maximum of 25 outpatient visits per year; the initial authorization was for 10 sessions, and the provider requested 15 more sessions. When a provider requests the balance of authorized sessions, the reviewer becomes suspicious about what is guiding treatment: goals or number of authorized sessions.

Based on your documentation, the reviewer can make one of the following decisions:

1. Authorize continued services.
2. Deny authorization of reimbursable services.
3. Defer for more information (you will be sent a letter inquiring about certain issues before further sessions are authorized).
4. Request a second opinion on the case.

The reviewer will take into account the reason why the referral was made, if any progress has been recorded, the provider's treatment strategy, and if the current status of the case warrants medically necessary services. Most importantly, the reviewer will be considering whether the money used for reimbursement of services is money well spent. If the reviewer feels the managed care system is not receiving a solid service for the money, the reviewer may exercise many options to insure that efficient and effective treatment is being delivered. Frequently, the first line of action is to communicate (verbally or through a letter) with the provider to get a better sense of what the provider is trying to accomplish. At this time the reviewer will remind the provider about the purpose of the referral and the philosophy of the managed care system (hints to the provider to consider a more directive therapy style).

Feldman (1992) used the phrase "constructive tension" to describe the effect that such dialogue about cases may create. This constructive tension, he believes, benefits the clients, but in order for it to work, the managed care system cannot assume too much control on the therapy process, and the provider must not be dependent on the financial income provided by the reimbursement of the managed care system. If providers become too dependent on the managed care system for referrals, then they may not engage in dialogue about cases, fearing a decrease in referrals. Feldman (1992) suggested that a private practice clinician not receive more than 15% to 20% of referrals from one managed care system.

Concurrent reviews may take on many different forms. Regardless of stylistic differences, it is simply best to keep your documentation behavioral and to the point, and to answer the questions asked.

The relationship between mental health professionals and managed mental health care systems has been strained. Many factors have contributed to this stressful relationship. Managed care systems have experimented, and continue to experiment, in service delivery so that more efficient and cost-effective services can be delivered. Some of the results of being cost-conscious include horrific stories of not hospitalizing when hospitalization was indicated and discontinuing services when services were needed. Mental health professionals contributed to the stressed relationship by not following the procedures outlined by the managed care system. Just as managed care systems are trying to improve their process of managing benefits, clinicians need to adjust their practice styles to be more in step with managed care systems.

FLEXIBLE THERAPEUTIC ATTITUDE

The days of service delivery in which a therapist works in isolation and can become a self-proclaimed expert are slowly fading. When working with managed care systems, you will need to interface with someone in the system, usually a case manager. A "prima donna" attitude will only alienate the case manager and create unproductive tension. Listen to the case manager's input and give it careful consideration before making a decision regarding the treatment you provide. Butler (1994) reported that many clinicians have not had a boss or needed to work in a collaborative manner with other professionals, and this adjustment is often painful. Good clinical work and a flexible attitude will establish you as a preferred provider, and it may gain you a reputation as an expert, whether you want the accolades or not.

QUALITY SERVICE DELIVERY

All mental health professionals feel they provide quality services. However, when working with a managed care system your services will be examined. Know your limitations! In the days of indemnity plans and cash-paying clients, if you took a referral for which you were unsure of your skills, no one noticed as long as the client simply maintained his or her condition or did not decompensate. A managed care system, on the other hand, wants to see change. Try to resist the temptation of taking every client referred to you by a managed care system, especially if you do not feel comfortable working with a certain population or diagnosis. It is better to turn down a referral and demonstrate you are aware of your limitations than to take a referral and get a bad reputation.

It is important at this time to acknowledge the difference between good clinicians and good managed care clinicians. There are many excellent clinicians who cannot or will not work for reduced rates, be kept accountable, practice a therapeutic style more oriented to symptom relief, or work with someone else in developing treatment plans. These clinicians may possess excellent clinical skills but may not be suited for a managed care practice. In contrast, there are clinicians who possess equally exceptional clinical skills and do not mind the managed care intrusion. It is possible to be a good clinician but not a good managed care clinician. Do you know what you are?

The following is a simple checklist to see if you could be a good managed care clinician. The more "Yes" responses you give, the better the managed care clinician you could be.

1. Are you organized enough to adjust to the multiple requirements of different managed care systems?

2. Can you live with a service delivery style emphasizing symptom relief?
3. Are you behavioral in your treatment style and/or description of treatment?
4. Can you accept suggestions from another clinician?
5. Are you comfortable with being held accountable for service delivery?
6. Are you comfortable with reporting your progress with the client?

With managed competition, it is going to be very important for mental health professionals to develop a research design for their practices. The research conducted by private practice clinicians and psychiatric hospitals will need to determine not only whether clients were satisfied with the services, but also that the service was effective. Mental health professionals will need to collect data from their clients on a regular basis (e.g., 3-, 6-, 9-month intervals) following the termination of treatment. The data will need to be compiled so that a clinician's effectiveness can be demonstrated to entities considering using their services.

CONSIDER A PRACTICE GROUP

Sometimes referred to as "Practice Without Walls" (*Managed Care News*, 1993), a practice group can be advantageous to both providers and managed care systems. Marketing and managed care relations are two advantages for a practice group. Marketing costs can be reduced. The entire group can share the costs of developing brochures and handouts that would typically be quite expensive for an individual provider. A second advantage is that managed care relations can be developed more efficiently. Instead of having to visit each managed care system on your own, each group member can be assigned as liaison to a different managed care system. The liaison can be responsible for announcing upcoming events for the group practice (e.g., communication skills training workshop), maintaining contact with key people in the system, and getting questions answered and processes clarified.

The advantage a practice group can offer a managed care system is more diverse services. Although you individually cannot provide services for all types of clients and diagnoses, your practice group will be able to provide many more services than you as an individual therapist. If possible, your group should include clinicians with overlapping skills so that a breadth of psychotherapy services can be offered (Cummings & VandenBos, 1978; Foos et al., 1991). It is more advantageous to have a group of clinicians offering services including medication management, family therapy, ability to work with geriatrics, and sex therapy than it is to have four clinicians who all specialize in family therapy. This range of services is attractive to managed care systems, especially if a constructive/cooperative relationship has been forged between the managed care system and the practice group.

When developing a practice group, some administrative qualities that should be present include (*Managed Care News*, 1993):

- providers with different geographic locations
- one telephone number for the group
- central billing
- emergency coverage
- outcome measures
- utilization statistics

Qualities of the practice group members should include the following:

- ability to be accountable for clinical outcomes
- cooperative with the group, a team player
- able to cope with business endeavors (e.g., capitated plans)
- competent members with a successful track record with managed care, *not* members who are friends or colleagues
- members with different degrees, licenses, and specialties

DEVELOP A BUSINESS ATTITUDE

A business attitude goes beyond developing a solid referral network which was customary prior to managed care. With the advent of managed care, even the most reliable referral sources will need to know if you are part of a network before they can make a referral to you. Some of the questions you will need to consider are:

- What is my business plan?
- How many managed care systems will I apply to per month?
- How will I identify managed care systems?
- After I am accepted to a system, whom do I contact?
- What is the proportion of clients I want from managed care?
- How often will I contact the managed care system for marketing purposes?

These questions are not entirely new to the practice of psychotherapy, but now mental health professionals need to be continuously aware of such issues. Mental health professionals need to become marketing agents, public relations specialists, and business strategists. Additionally, they will need to live by the motto of "marketing or morbidity" (Cummings & Duhl, 1987).

Businesses constantly assess their market status, product line, and internal strengths and weaknesses. Likewise, mental health professionals need to become sophisticated at monitoring and continuously assessing their practice status in regard to market expectations. The technology, administratively and clinically, is rapidly changing. Clinicians need to find innovative methods to track and record when concurrent reviews are due, have methods to transmit and receive information instantaneously, and be able to have organized charts in the event an audit is requested. See Appendix E (pp. 79-85) for "Managed Care Practice Assessments" (Outpatient Practice/Practice Group vs. Structured Outpatient Facility/Program).

WORK FOR A MANAGED CARE SYSTEM

When a managed care system establishes itself in a community, it often needs to acquire contracted therapists and consultants. Contracted therapists often provide psychotherapy, assessment, and referral services. Although becoming a contracted therapist is not as lucrative as being a network provider, it can provide excellent training in how a managed care system works. Additionally, being a contracted therapist establishes you as a credible clinician who knows about managed care so at a later date, when you become a network provider, you already have a positive reputation within the system. Foos et al. (1991) reported that working for a managed care company can equip therapists with some skills that enable them to establish a company operated by mental health professionals.

Another possible position to consider within a managed care system is as a consultant. Managed care systems often need someone to provide group consultations for their own therapists or to give an opinion regarding difficult and complex cases. If you become a consultant in a limited capacity, you may gain a positive reputation within the system and learn the "nuts and bolts" of how that managed care system operates.

KEEP UP-TO-DATE

Try to keep up-to-date regarding the research in your areas of interest. By keeping current you may be viewed as the expert in that area and asked to provide training to the clinicians in the managed care system. Keeping up-to-date also demonstrates your commitment to the field.

ADDITIONAL TRAINING

Managed care systems adhere to the assumptions and clinical practices of brief therapy. They follow the research, or conduct it themselves, on the effectiveness of brief therapy with mental and behavioral health issues. Foos et al. (1991) emphasized the necessity of clinicians needing to stay current with the most efficient and effective psychotherapy models. I applied to a managed care system, had been accepted, and requested a meeting with a representative from the system. During our discussion, this representative asked me if I was aware of the brief therapy model of William O'Hanlon and Michele Weiner-Davis (1989), because that was the style of therapy they wanted their network providers to follow. Fortunately, I was able to say "Yes."

If you are unfamiliar with brief therapy or are uncomfortable with the style, it will be beneficial for you to receive some training in this area. Be sure you get a signed certificate of completion after attending any training that a managed care system would find beneficial for its network. This certificate will be good documentation to submit with your application to the managed care system.

IDEALISTIC GOALS

Traditionally, psychotherapy service delivery has not been monitored, with the result that clinicians sometimes have become a confidant/consultant to clients for seemingly minor issues. Often the boundary is crossed between an active therapeutic process, with specific problems to be solved, and personal growth and development. Within a managed care system, personal growth and development usually do not indicate medical necessity. Therefore, such services will not be reimbursed. Clinicians must adapt to and create a therapy climate that solves the presented problem rather than striving for an idealistic goal. Striving for such a goal is acceptable, but clinicians must recognize that such services may not be reimbursable.

TREATMENT IS THEORY DRIVEN

One of the seven illusions of psychotherapy is unanimity (Furman & Ahola, 1988). Psychotherapists forget that they usually associate with clinicians who have similar views regarding mental health issues. The result is that when a new theory is introduced, clinicians often disqualify it because it does not fit with their "truth." When working with managed care systems it is important that you remember your theory is not more accurate or inaccurate than the case manager's. Of course, the case manager should also keep this in mind. If you accept the truth of this illusion, a more cooperative relationship can be created with the managed care system because you will not have to prove each of your world-views.

DIVERSIFICATION

Clinicians will need to diversify their service delivery. Some clinicians may be able to support their practices solely on service delivery, but it will become increasingly difficult. Clinicians need to identify where they can utilize their clinical skills and knowledge, and try to develop another area of their practice. Curtis (1988) described his career change from marriage and family therapy to organizational consulting and emphasized how his skills were transferable. Other examples include training other clinicians in your area of expertise, lecturing, consultation, or teaching. I attended a seminar at a state conference in which the clinician discussed how to develop a consulting practice with specific populations unrelated to the field of mental health. Psychotherapy skills can be used in many areas. Why not use them for something other than psychotherapy?

Chapter 7

Impacted Disciplines

Foos et al. (1991) reported that all mental health disciplines will need to make adjustments, but probably the discipline that will need to make the biggest adjustment is psychiatry. Psychiatrists are in a very precarious position. Their session rates for psychotherapy services are usually much higher than those of other disciplines. Unless they are highly specialized or the service includes a medical component, a managed care system will most likely refer to a mental health professional who can provide quality talk therapy services at a lesser rate. There is no reason for a managed care company to pay $120 per session for psychotherapy services (nonmedical), when another equally qualified clinician will provide the same service for $60 per session. Another area impacted in a psychiatrist's practice is supervision. Psychiatrists have often been used as supervisors for other clinicians so that clinicians could receive third-party payment. Managed care systems typically require a provider to be licensed, but usually do not require that they be supervised by a psychiatrist; psychiatrists will need to adjust to this financial decrease in their practice.

More than ever, psychiatrists will need to make the adjustment of diversification. The fact that similar services can be offered by other disciplines at a lower rate does not mean psychiatrists are not needed. For example, psychiatrists who have exceptional knowledge regarding medication management can be used on cases in conjunction with another therapist. Furthermore, psychiatrists can assist with second opinions and case consultation with complex cases. Psychiatry will be forced to consider how it wants to be involved with managed care systems, and psychiatrists will have to consider a number of options: reduce rates, become highly specialized with complex diagnoses, develop a medication management practice, or build a consulting practice.

Psychologists, social workers, marriage and family therapists, and other mental health disciplines will be impacted adversely if they do not adjust to the competitive nature of the mental health business. The range of mental health disciplines typically has not been trained or exposed to such business concepts of planning and marketing. It will become imperative to acquire such skills and knowledge in order to survive in a managed care world.

At the grass-roots level, universities and training programs will need to take more responsibility for helping students become better prepared for careers in mental health. Regardless of where students begin their careers (e.g., EAPs, managed care systems, hospitals, universities, or mental health centers), they will be exposed to managed mental health care concepts and practices, and time-limited therapy. Students will need to be informed about managed care and have some training in brief therapy; it would also not be detrimental to take some business courses.

Although it will be necessary for universities and training programs to continue to expose students to the broad range of clinical theory and practice, students will need knowledge and skills that will make them competitive in the job market. During a lecture I gave to students and professionals on brief therapy, questions were asked about managed care. Following the lecture, some students who were about to graduate from their program approached me to inquire how they could gain more information and experience in managed care and brief therapy. These students expressed shock, anger, and surprise that they had been exposed to brief therapy concepts only in a superficial manner, and that they had not been exposed to any managed mental health care issues. A single lecture or chapter from a book on either of these topics is simply not enough to prepare students for the job market that awaits them.

Chapter 9

The Role of Employee Assistance Programs

Employee assistance programs (EAPs) are increasingly playing a major role in managed mental health services. EAPs which have capital, clinical knowledge, and an information system in place are beginning to grow into managed mental health companies themselves. Furthermore, managed care systems are increasingly developing their own EAPs to offer to client companies. This expansion of services by both systems can be beneficial to clinicians who are comfortable in delivering time-limited therapy.

As EAPs expand and develop managed care services for companies, clinicians who have a good working relationship with the EAP will be in a good position to become preferred providers within the managed care system. These EAPs will not want to experiment with new providers when the transition to managed care is made.

Typically, only an external EAP will be in a position to do managed care. However, this does not mean that internal EAPs should be forgotten. If a business should decide to utilize managed care and it has an internal EAP, the internal EAP will usually have significant influence in the type of managed care package chosen. Additionally, if a system is chosen that utilizes a network of some sort, the internal EAP may be in a position to suggest the providers that are most useful for the company.

Another significant role for EAPs involves joint ventures of free-standing EAPs with managed care systems. In the hypothetical example regarding the GeeWhiz Widget Corporation, ABC

Managed Care Company could have joined forces with a free-standing EAP; together they could have placed a bid into Gee-Whiz to manage the mental health benefits. Such joint ventures will continue to increase between quality EAPs and managed care systems.

The role of EAPs in managed care is going to increase. It will be to your benefit to continue a positive relationship with any EAPs you associate with, and begin to develop further EAP referral sources.

During consultations with practice groups and agencies, some questions come up repeatedly. By addressing the following issues, providers can begin to make many of the needed adaptations to work more cooperatively with the managed care system.

Question: I'm currently a provider in a network. How do I get some referrals?

Answer: Develop a brochure or flyer and send it to the network. Request a meeting in which you can market your practice and educate the system about how you can help it deliver a quality service and save it money. Try to identify who is in charge of making referrals and meet with these people or at least talk with them on the telephone.

Question: I'm not in any provider networks. Where do I start?

Answer: Network with clinicians who are in networks. These clinicians may know of a developing or open network. Try to attend meetings that are sponsored by managed care systems and inquire if you can apply.

Question: I feel I can make the necessary adjustments to work with managed care/competition. What should I do to best adjust my practice?

Answer: Three things would best position you to deal with managed care/competition: First, acquire a state-of-the-art communications system. Consider using voice mail with an automatic pager system so you are made aware of all messages immediately. Second, should you choose to work aggressively with managed care/competition, your paperwork demands will assuredly increase. You may want to invest in a computer system so that you can store the required managed care forms. You can also store treatment data without having to rewrite by hand all information (e.g., concurrent review information). Finally, set up your practice to have a thorough research and follow-up design. Such a design will be important to any entity considering contracting with you for services.

Question: I have worked with managed care systems and I often hear the phrase "medically necessary services." Would you please explain what this phrase means?

Answer: Usually, the phrase "medically necessary services" refers to how the client is impacted. Medically necessary means that some major life function (work, family, social) of an individual has been impaired by the presented problem. For example, services for someone who is depressed and is not attending work due to the depression would be deemed medically necessary. On the other hand, someone who is adjusting to a recent relocation, is experiencing some depressed symptoms, but is continuing to work and socialize may not fit the definition of medically necessary.

Question: I need to complete a concurrent review. What should I emphasize?

Answer: Emphasize in behavioral terms the presented problem, treatment plan, and termination criteria.

Question: My private practice is shrinking and I need to do something with managed care. What should I do?

Answer: A number of options are available. Consider if you want to work for a managed care system as a consultant or contract employee. Start to develop a marketing plan that can stimulate referrals if you are already part of some networks. If you are not participating in any networks, begin to identify and apply to any networks you can. Another possibility is to consider your strengths and try to apply your knowledge and skills to other areas. You may want to begin training in an area of expertise, begin consulting with organizations, give lectures, or teach.

Question: There is no way I can meet all clinicians within one managed care system, not to mention other systems. How do I get my name recognized?

Answer: Develop a marketing brochure or flyer that you can periodically mail out to managed care systems. This marketing effort will keep you visible to clinicians and systems without your needing to make direct contact with each person within the system.

Question: I have been told that the network is closed; is there a way to get accepted?

Answer: Possibly, provided you have a specific skill that the network lacks, for example, competence in American Sign Language. Another way to get into the network may exist if you can demonstrate how you will provide quality services and save the managed care system money. Finally, knowing someone in the system who has the influence to get you an application may get you into the network.

Question: I know I do good work, but it does not seem like the managed care system agrees with me, and I am afraid I will lose them as a referral source. What can I do?

Answer: If you are suspicious of the managed care system's perception of you, try to arrange a meeting with someone within the system to "clear the air."

Question: Pastors have been great referral sources, but they now need to know what provider lists I am on. Can I give them such a list?

Answer: Generally, yes. However, you should make sure that in the contract you signed with the managed care system there is not a clause forbidding such action. You may want to contact the system directly to clarify the issue and get a response in writing.

Question: I believe short-term counseling is a Band-Aid approach and managed care does not allow for true healing to occur. I know I need to work with the system to keep my practice, but I do not agree with the practice orientation. What can I do?

Answer: You may fall into the category of being a great clinician but not a great managed care clinician. I would suggest finding other referral sources that do not have the managed care limitations or consider diversifying yourself.

Question: It appears that, with the advent of managed care and competition, the profession of psychotherapy is diminishing. Is the profession shrinking?

Answer: It is possible that the number of professionals in private practice is decreasing. As the practice of groups without walls continues to expand, more and more individuals may be leaving or not entering the private practice area. In sales there is a saying that 20% of the sales force makes 80% of the money. This saying may indicate the trend for private practitioners. On the bright side, however, more job opportunities are being created as the sophistication of managed care increases. Psychiatric hospitals are hiring clinicians experienced in brief therapy as psychotherapists, case managers, and liaisons to managed care companies. Managed care companies are hiring inpatient and outpatient utilization reviewers, case managers, and specialized clinicians to deliver focused treatment. The career opportunities are definitely expanding beyond the traditional view of psychotherapy.

Question: I am a member of a PPO, and the managed care system has expanded to include EAP work. Should I do anything different?

Answer: Because you do not know the specific EAP model or the type of clientele that may be generated, it would be a good idea to make contact with someone within the system (by phone or in person) to clarify how the EAP may change the referral process and type of client.

Question: A managed care system I am a provider for authorizes in increments of only three sessions, and then I must submit a new concurrent review. Is there anything I can do to cut down on the paperwork?

Answer: Yes. Take the time to create the concurrent review form on your computer (if you have one) and complete the form using your computer. This process will save handwriting or typing time, and through the "cut and paste" technology of computers you will not need to rewrite many sections.

Question: I try to allot $500 per year for training. What type of training do you suggest?

Answer: Any training that demonstrates you have knowledge about managed care systems and brief therapy. If you are having difficulty getting into systems, or have seen a decrease in referrals, I suggest at least 20 hours of training in brief therapy or managed care. It will be important to get certificates of completion so that you can enclose them with your application.

Question: I am a student in a graduate counseling program. What can I do to better prepare myself for the competitive job market?

Answer: Try to get a practicum or internship with a managed care system or an EAP. The experience will be priceless. Training in brief therapy is imperative.

Question: How can we make our group practice more appealing to a managed care system?

Answer: Create overlapping services so that your group can be considered for a variety of clientele. Additionally, without good relations with the managed care system, it will not matter what you offer for services, so try to forge a cooperative relationship with the system.

Question: Can my private practice survive without participating in managed mental health care?

Answer: Yes, but you will need to diversify your practice to possibly include training and consultation, and you will need to develop a very strong reputation so that people will choose you over the financial considerations they must make.

Chapter 11

Conclusion

The field of psychotherapy has seen many changes in recent years, and these changes will continue throughout the remainder of the decade. Mental health professionals have typically been one-dimensional. They have relied too heavily on their clinical skills as their lifeline. Today, clinicians need to have many skills covering such areas as administration, marketing, research, and communications. As the field continues to mature, so must clinicians.

We have all seen clients who had difficulty with a change in job position or a break in a family tradition. Typically, we help them to define how they can adapt to the new work environment or try to establish new family traditions. As we know, the changes will occur regardless of how reluctant our clients are.

We, too, are now faced with a major challenge to our job, career, and traditions in practice and profession. It is imperative that we disengage from a victim's role and begin to mobilize ourselves into a mental position of survivorship. To accomplish this paradigm shift we need to view these changes as challenges and opportunities.

Appendices

APPENDIX A

SAMPLE MARKETING LETTER

Center for Effective Treatment
5678 Brief Avenue, D-100
Westminster, CO 00000

June 1, 1994

Dr. John Smith
XYZ Health Systems
1234 Clark Avenue, #567
Denver, CO 00000

Dear Dr. Smith:

The Center for Effective Treatment would like to apply for inclusion in your provider network. Although your network may be closed, we feel the Center for Effective Treatment can help meet your clinical as well as financial objectives.

The mission of the Center for Effective Treatment (CET) is to provide quality mental and behavioral health services in a time-limited manner. The goal of the psychotherapy provided at the CET is to help clients become more self-sufficient and recognize their own abilities and solutions in dealing with problematic situations. In 1993 our mean number of sessions for all clinicians was 4.11. We utilize a database system that measures the average number of sessions per diagnosis, cost per treatment episode, and client satisfaction. As a benefit to our contracted companies, we provide semiannual reports on these and other variables.

At the Center for Effective Treatment we are in a position to meet your clinical objectives by providing quality service delivery, and your financial objective by using time-limited therapy. We cordially request four applications for inclusion in your network. Please feel free to call us at (303) 555-1111 if you have any further questions.

Sincerely,

Tracy Todd, PhD, LMFT

APPENDIX B

TEN QUESTIONS TO ASK
THE MANAGED CARE SYSTEM

1. How can I meet your clinical objective?

2. How can I meet your financial objective?

3. What type of psychotherapy service does your network lack?

4. How many lives does your network cover?

5. How many clinicians work for your system locally?

6. How does the referral system operate?

7. How many sessions are internal clinicians allowed before needing to refer?

8. What is the rough percentage of referrals you make to your network?

9. If I accept a referral, what is the process I should follow?

10. What is the managed care systems's philosophy toward service delivery?

APPENDIX C

CHECKLIST FOR BILLING CONSIDERATIONS

1. Have you received authorization to provide psychotherapy (check one)? ☐Yes ☐No

2. If yes, what is the authorization date? _____
    Number? _____

3. What is the process if I need more sessions?

4. When do I start this process if needed?

5. When should I submit my bills?

6. To whom do I submit the bills?

7. What should be included on the bill?

8. What is the copayment for the client?

9. When should the copayment be collected?

10. What is the deductible for the client?

11. Can I bill the client (check one)? ☐Yes ☐No

12. Under what circumstances can the client be billed?

APPENDIX D

WEAK CONCURRENT REVIEW

Outpatient Concurrent Review Form

Name: Jeff Jones   **Case Number:** 5319
SS#: 000-00-0000   **Date First Seen:** 2-1-92
Number of Sessions to Date: 8
Diagnosis: 296

Assessment: Jeff appears to be a depressed individual who grew up in a family in which there was strict discipline and lack of a positive role model differentiating work and play. Subsequently, Jeff has repressed his playful personality. His son's needs to interact with Jeff seem to be overwhelming Jeff, and until Jeff can learn to be playful the depression will continue.

Treatment Plan and Goals: We will hold weekly meetings that explore family-of-origin issues so that Jeff can gain insight into how these issues are influencing his repressed exuberance for life and, in turn, contributing to his depression. After Jeff has gained significant insight into his condition, which he is beginning to do, we will explore the appropriate ways for him to express his playfulness and hopefully lift his depression. The goal will be for Jeff to be able to enjoy his sense of self and family, and to confront his parents so that family-of-origin issues can finally be resolved.

Response to Treatment: Jeff is beginning to develop a trusting relationship with me. Because he is not a very insightful person, it is taking considerable time to get him to understand how his family-of-origin issues and repression influence his depression. He continues to miss approximately 2 days of work per week which indicates the significance of his depression. He is cooperative in the therapy process.

Termination Criteria: I am unable to assess when treatment will be concluded. The termination process will begin after Jeff understands how his childhood experiences limit his ability to have fun and after he has resolved these issues with his parents. No foreseeable termination date is seen at this time.

Additional Sessions Needed: 15

Comments: None

STRONG CONCURRENT REVIEW

Outpatient Concurrent Review Form

Name: Jeff Jones   **Case Number:** 5319
SS#: 000-00-0000   **Date First Seen:** 2-1-92
Number of Sessions to Date: 8
Diagnosis: 296.22 (Major depression, single episode, moderate)
         defer
         none reported
         3 (moderate)
         60 (current)
         75 (past year)

Assessment: Jeff is a 32-year-old male, married 5 years, with a 2-year-old son. Marriage is solid, but financial stressors due to decreased work attendance has created some tension. It seems Jeff is a hard worker (confirmed by supervisor), but he has not taken any vacation time in the last 3 years to enjoy himself. His vacations include such activities as working on the house or yard and visiting relatives. Jeff does not have any daily or weekly activities he can participate in for enjoyment. His wife is supportive of the therapy process. The symptoms of depression exhibited are loss of interest in pleasurable activities, fatigue, feelings of guilt, decreased concentration, and insomnia.

Treatment Plan and Goals: Frequency of meetings is currently two sessions per month. We will be moving to monthly meetings when Jeff is not missing work due to depression. Utilizing wife in therapy process for support and consultation. Focusing on developing stress-relieving activities on a daily and weekly basis. Will consult with Jeff's supervisor about his improvement in work performance (release of information has been signed). Goals for Jeff are:

1. Identify and participate in one daily activity he finds enjoyable
2. Identify and participate in two weekly activities he finds enjoyable
3. Improved work attendance, no absences related to depression

Response to Treatment: Jeff has responded well to establishing treatment goals and engaging in stress-relieving activities. He is missing about 1 day of work every 2 weeks due to depression. He has identified his daily activity for stress relief as a 30-minute walk in the evening. His identified weekly activities are 2 hours of woodworking and a family activity (movies, dinner, etc.).

Termination Criteria:

1. No missed work due to depression in 30 days
2. No depressive symptoms for 30 days that result in adverse consequences (job jeopardy, marital conflict)
3. A Global Assessment of Functioning (GAF) score of 75 will determine termination of therapy with a follow-up session scheduled 2 months later.

Additional Sessions Needed: 8; will continue meeting with Jeff every 2 to 4 weeks until termination criteria are met. Will have one follow-up session 2 months later.

Comments: None

APPENDIX E

MANAGED CARE PRACTICE ASSESSMENT

Outpatient Practice/Practice Group

The purpose of this assessment is to determine how attractive your practice or practice group would be to a managed care company. The more "Yes" responses, the more attractive your practice. Those variables viewed as anticipating future demands which would be especially positive in marketing your practice, have been given an asterisk (*).

Coverage

Yes ____ No ____ 24 hour/7 day emergency system
Yes ____ No ____ Medical backup
Yes ____ No ____ Admitting privileges at a network hospital
Yes ____ No ____ Available for crisis sessions within 24 hours
Yes ____ No ____ Out-of-town coverage system
Yes ____ No ____ Available to respond to crisis calls within 60 minutes
Yes ____ No ____ Available to respond to crisis calls within 20 minutes (more favorable)

Services

Yes ____ No ____ Individual therapy
Yes ____ No ____ Family therapy
Yes ____ No ____ Group therapy (current)
Yes ____ No ____ Psychological testing
Yes ____ No ____ Psychological assessments (e.g., Beck's depression)
Yes ____ No ____ Able to admit involuntary clients to facilities

Performance

Yes ____ No ____ *Average number of sessions < 10
Yes ____ No ____ Recommended by network MD
Yes ____ No ____ Recommended by network provider (for MDs)

*Database System

Yes ____ No ____ Measure number of sessions
Yes ____ No ____ Track diagnoses treated
Yes ____ No ____ Revenue collected per case

Database System *(Cont'd)*

Yes _____   No _____   Generate reports
Yes _____   No _____   Sort managed care companies
Yes _____   No _____   Track client satisfaction
Yes _____   No _____   Monitor outcome measures

Computer Literate

Yes _____   No _____   Can create database system
Yes _____   No _____   Use of electronic bulletin boards
Yes _____   No _____   Generate reports

Multidisciplinary

Yes _____   No _____   MD
Yes _____   No _____   PhD/PsyD
Yes _____   No _____   MSW
Yes _____   No _____   MA/MS
Yes _____   No _____   RN
Yes _____   No _____   CAC

Multilicensed

Yes _____   No _____   Licensed Marriage and Family Therapist
Yes _____   No _____   Licensed Psychiatrist
Yes _____   No _____   Licensed Psychologist
Yes _____   No _____   Licensed Professional Counselor
Yes _____   No _____   Licensed Clinical Social Worker

*Training

Yes _____   No _____   20+ hours of brief therapy training
Yes _____   No _____   10+ hours of managed care training
Yes _____   No _____   Previous managed care experience/training
Yes _____   No _____   Employee assistance experience/training
Yes _____   No _____   Multicultural training
Yes _____   No _____   Bilingual

Office

Yes _____   No _____   Separate entrance/exit
Yes _____   No _____   Handicapped accessible
Yes _____   No _____   Public transportation within 1 block
Yes _____   No _____   Telecommunications Device for the Deaf (TDD)
Yes _____   No _____   Private waiting area
Yes _____   No _____   FAX capabilities

Hours Available

Yes _____ No _____ Monday - Friday 7 a.m. - 5 p.m.
Yes _____ No _____ Monday 5 p.m. - 9 p.m.
Yes _____ No _____ Tuesday 5 p.m. - 9 p.m.
Yes _____ No _____ Wednesday 5 p.m. - 9 p.m.
Yes _____ No _____ Thursday 5 p.m. - 9 p.m.
Yes _____ No _____ *Friday 5 p.m. - 9 p.m.
Yes _____ No _____ *Saturday 7 a.m. - 5 p.m.
Yes _____ No _____ Sunday 7 a.m. - 5 p.m.

Liability Coverage

Yes _____ No _____ Personal injury
Yes _____ No _____ Malpractice
Yes _____ No _____ All other applicable insurance

Treatment Planning

Yes _____ No _____ Behavioral treatment plans
Yes _____ No _____ Termination criteria (measurable)
Yes _____ No _____ Closing summaries (database information)
Yes _____ No _____ Internal quality assurance system
Yes _____ No _____ *Internal utilization review of cases with 8+ sessions
Yes _____ No _____ Peer supervision/consultation
Yes _____ No _____ Resource catalog of community supports
Yes _____ No _____ *Client satisfaction survey

MANAGED CARE PRACTICE ASSESSMENT

<u>Structured Outpatient Facility/Program*</u>

In determining the attractiveness of a structured outpatient facility or program, many variables can be assessed, ranging from clinical designs to pricing structures. Please keep in mind that no one program will satisfy all the criteria listed. However, the more sophisticated a facility or program, the more attractive it will appear to managed care systems. Those variables viewed as anticipating future demands have been given an asterisk (*).

<u>Admissions</u>

Yes _____ No _____ *Detox services, in-house
Yes _____ No _____ *Detox services, immediate access/admissions
Yes _____ No _____ Staff MD
Yes _____ No _____ Antabuse/medication monitoring
Yes _____ No _____ *24-hour admissions
Yes _____ No _____ *Dual track for treatment of substance abuse and mental health

<u>Programs Available For</u>

Yes _____ No _____ Adults
Yes _____ No _____ Adolescents
Yes _____ No _____ In-house urine screens
Yes _____ No _____ In-house psychological/neuropsychological testing
Yes _____ No _____ *Substance-specific programs (e.g., prescription, narcotics)
Yes _____ No _____ Accredited by representative body

<u>Individual Programming</u>

Yes _____ No _____ 12-Step
Yes _____ No _____ *Rational recovery or other treatment modality
Yes _____ No _____ *Bilingual
Yes _____ No _____ Family involvement
Yes _____ No _____ Structured aftercare
Yes _____ No _____ *Family aftercare

---

*Developed by Scott Rosthauser, MC, Licensed Professional Counselor. He is an inpatient/ structured outpatient utilization review specialist for a managed mental health care company. Reprinted by permission.

Weekend Programming
Yes _____ No _____ Comprehensive treatment delivery
Yes _____ No _____ Ability to facilitate employer/employee demands
(i.e., no disruption of work schedule)
Yes _____ No _____ Individualized programming (i.e., ability to make
transition from weekday to weekend program with
continuity of care)
Yes _____ No _____ Access to random urine screens

*Return To Work Component
Yes _____ No _____ Can interface with workplace
Yes _____ No _____ Can interface with employee assistance program
Yes _____ No _____ Fitness for duty experience
Yes _____ No _____ Case management for mandated follow-up
Yes _____ No _____ Urine screens for mandated length of time

Relapse Program
Yes _____ No _____ Family involvement
Yes _____ No _____ 24-hour admission
Yes _____ No _____ Longer phase aftercare
Yes _____ No _____ Workplace involvement
Yes _____ No _____ *Can reenter treatment at appropriate developmen-
tal program sequence

*Database System
Yes _____ No _____ Measure relapse rate
Yes _____ No _____ Track diagnoses treated
Yes _____ No _____ Revenue collected per case
Yes _____ No _____ Generate reports
Yes _____ No _____ Sort managed care companies
Yes _____ No _____ Track client satisfaction
Yes _____ No _____ Monitor outcome measures

Computer Literate
Yes _____ No _____ Can create database system
Yes _____ No _____ Use of electronic bulletin boards
Yes _____ No _____ Generate reports

Multidisciplinary
Yes _____ No _____ MD
Yes _____ No _____ PhD/PsyD
Yes _____ No _____ MSW
Yes _____ No _____ MA/MS
Yes _____ No _____ RN

Multilicensed

Yes _____   No _____   Licensed Marriage and Family Therapist
Yes _____   No _____   Licensed Psychiatrist
Yes _____   No _____   Licensed Psychologist
Yes _____   No _____   Licensed Professional Counselor
Yes _____   No _____   Licensed Clinical Social Worker
Yes _____   No _____   Certified Alcohol/Drug Counselors

*Training

Yes _____   No _____   20+ hours of solution-based training
Yes _____   No _____   10+ hours of managed care training
Yes _____   No _____   Previous managed care experience/training
Yes _____   No _____   Employee assistance experience/training
Yes _____   No _____   Multicultural training
Yes _____   No _____   Bilingual
Yes _____   No _____   Addictions training, specific to substance
Yes _____   No _____   Detox specific training

Office

Yes _____   No _____   Multiple locations of service delivery
Yes _____   No _____   Handicapped accessible
Yes _____   No _____   Public transportation within 1 block
Yes _____   No _____   Telecommunications Device for the Deaf (TDD)
Yes _____   No _____   *Ability to monitor same gender urine screens
Yes _____   No _____   FAX capabilities

Hours

Yes _____   No _____   Intake/assessment 24-hour capabilities
Yes _____   No _____   Interchangeable day, evening, weekend programming
Yes _____   No _____   Urine screens available 6 a.m. - 10 p.m.

Liability Coverage

Yes _____   No _____   Personal injury
Yes _____   No _____   Malpractice
Yes _____   No _____   Individual professional

Treatment Planning

Yes _____   No _____   Familiar with admission/discharge criteria by sanctioning body
Yes _____   No _____   *Initial report following admission within 48 hours
Yes _____   No _____   Behavioral treatment plans
Yes _____   No _____   Termination criteria (measurable)

Treatment Planning *(Cont'd)*

Yes _____ No _____ Closing summaries (database information)
Yes _____ No _____ Internal quality assurance system
Yes _____ No _____ *Internal utilization review of cases at transition points
Yes _____ No _____ Internal/external supervision/consultation
Yes _____ No _____ Resource catalog of community supports
Yes _____ No _____ *Client satisfaction survey
Yes _____ No _____ Clear discharge plan
Yes _____ No _____ Documentation of follow-up
Yes _____ No _____ *Employer satisfaction survey
Yes _____ No _____ *Telephone access to assignment of random urine screen

References and Resources

CITED REFERENCES

Bacon, J. (1991). The challenges in mental health care benefits [Special Report]. *Business & Health,* 7-12.

Butler, K. (1994). Surviving the revolution. *Family Therapy Networker, 18,* 28-29.

Coile, R. C. (1992, January 10). Better get used to it: Managed care poised to absolutely rule the early 1990s. *Health Care Competition Week.*

Cummings, N. A., & Duhl, L. (1987). The new delivery system. In L. J. Duhl & N. Cummings (Eds.), *The Future of Mental Health Services: Coping with Crisis* (pp. 85-98). New York: Springer.

Cummings, N. A., & VandenBos, G. (1978). The general practice of psychology. *Professional Psychology, 10,* 430-440.

Curtis, J. (1988). Organization consulting: Keeping afloat in a larger pond. *The Family Therapy Networker, 12,* 19.

Feldman, S. (1992). Managed mental health services: Ideas and issues. In S. Feldman (Ed.), *Managed Mental Health Services* (pp. 3-26). Springfield, IL: Charles C. Thomas.

Foos, J., Ottens, A., & Hill, L. (1991). Managed mental health: A primer for counselors. *Journal of Counseling & Development, 69,* 332-336.

Furman, B., & Ahola, T. (1988). Seven illusions. *The Family Therapy Networker, 12,* 30-31.

Kunnes, R. (1992). Managed mental health: The insurer's perspective. In S. Feldman (Ed.), *Managed Mental Health Services* (pp. 101-125). Springfield, IL: Charles C. Thomas.

Managed Care News. (1993, June). Report from Psychotherapy Finances Managed Care Conference, Palm Beach, FL.

O'Hanlon, W. H., & Weiner-Davis, M. (1989). *In Search of Solutions: A New Direction in Psychotherapy.* New York: W. W. Norton.

Penzer, W. N. (1990). The realities of managed mental health care. *EAP Digest, 7,* 35-43.

Raso, L. (1993). Search for solutions. *The Journal of the American Association of the Preferred Provider Organization, 3,* 15-21.

ADDITIONAL RESOURCES

PUBLICATIONS

Behavioral Healthcare Tomorrow. Subscribe through Centralink, 1110 Mar West Street, Suite E, Tiburon, CA 94920-9928.

Business & Health. This journal is available from Medical Economics Publishing, 5 Paragon Drive, Montvale, NJ 07645.

The Exchange. Published by the Employee Assistance Professionals Association, Inc., 2101 Wilson Boulevard, Suite 500, Arlington, VA 22201; Telephone: (703) 522-6272.

Feldman, S. (1992). *Managed Mental Health Services.* Springfield, IL: Charles C. Thomas.

Giles, T. (1993). *Managed Mental Health Care: A Guide for Practitioners, Employers, and Hospital Administrators.* Boston: Allyn & Bacon.

The Journal of the American Association of Preferred Provider Organizations. This journal is available through Health Care Communications, One Bridge Plaza, Suite 350, Fort Lee, NJ 07024; Telephone: (201) 947-5545.

Managed Care: A Guide for Physicians. Available through Stezzi Communication Inc., 301 Oxford Valley Road, Suite 603-B, Yardley, PA 19067.

Managed Care Handbook. Published by Ridgewood Financial Institute, Inc., 1016 Clemons Street, Suite 407, Jupiter, FL 33477; Telephone: (800) 869-8450.

Patient Outcomes in Managed Care Settings. Available through Williams & Wilkins, 428 East Preston Street, Baltimore, MD 21202-3993; Telephone: (800) 443-5826, ext. 601.

Psychotherapy Finances. Published by Ridgewood Financial Institute, Inc., 1016 Clemons Street, Suite 407, Jupiter, FL 33477; Telephone: (800) 869-8450. Psychotherapy Finances also publishes the *Managed Care Strategies* newsletter and the *Guide to Private Practice*, and both can be obtained through the same address and telephone number.

Todd, T., & Hill, G. (1994). *Managed Care in the 90s.* Videotaped presentation produced by the Learning Edge Series™ of the American Association for Marriage and Family Therapy.

ASSOCIATIONS

American Association of Preferred Provider Organizations (AAPPO), 401 North Michigan Avenue, Chicago, IL 60611-4267; Telephone: (312) 644-6610. This industry trade group will send you its bimonthly newsletter, *Perspectives,* for $125 a year. It also sponsors the bimonthly *AAPPO Journal,* available for $35 per year from Health Care Communications, One Bridge Plaza, Suite 350, Fort Lee, NJ 07024. Ask to be on the mailing list for brochures listing new managed care studies as they are published.

American Managed Care Review Association (AMCRA), 25th Street, NW, Suite 610, Washington, DC 20037; Telephone: (202) 728-0506. AMCRA is a trade group representing a mixed bag of managed care; including HMOs, PPOs, IPAs, and peer review groups. For $195 they'll send you a complete directory of HMOs and PPOs, including good general and legal information. To follow industry trends, the AMCRA newsletter, *Monitor,* can be ordered at $120 for an annual subscription of eight issues.

Index

A

Administrative costs, 5
Administrative fees plan, 11
Application to a system, 27-33
Assessment, 41
Assessments, practice, 77-85
Associations, managed care, 89
Attitude,
    business, 48-49
    therapeutic, 45-46

B

Brief therapy, 7, 18, 21, 23, 32, 50-51, 55, 62, 63
Business news, 26

C

Capitated "at risk" benefit plan, 10
    example of, 20-23
Capitation, 10
Carve-out, 9
Case management, 9
Case manager, 45

G

Gender issues, 28
Geographic location, 30
Goals, 41-42, 51
Group model managed care system, 12
Group therapy, 30

H

Health Maintenance Organization, 3, 11-12
HMO (*see* Health Maintenance Organization)
Hospital services, 9, 16-17, 21
Hybrid model, 12-13
    example of, 15-20

I

Indemnification, mutual, 33
Internship, 63

J

Job postings, 25

L

Legal reform, 5-6
License, 29

M

Managed competition, 5-6
Marketing, 49, 61
    sample letter, 69

Add A Colleague To Our Mailing List . . .

If you would like us to send our latest catalog to one of your colleagues, please return this form.

Name:_____
       (Please Print)

Address:_____

Address:_____

City/State/Zip:_____

Telephone:(_____)_____

I am a:

_____ Psychologist   _____ Mental Health Counselor
_____ Psychiatrist   _____ Marriage and Family Therapist
_____ School Psychologist   _____ Not in Mental Health Field
_____ Clinical Social Worker   _____ Other:_____

◆   ◆   ◆

Professional Resource Press
P.O. Box 15560
Sarasota, FL 34277-1560

Telephone #941-366-7913
FAX #941-366-7971

If You Found This Book Useful . . .

You might want to know more about our other titles.

If you would like to receive our latest catalog, please return this form:

Name:_____
(Please Print)

Address:_____

Address:_____

City/State/Zip:_____

Telephone:(_____)_____

I am a:

_____ Psychologist   _____ Mental Health Counselor
_____ Psychiatrist   _____ Marriage and Family Therapist
_____ School Psychologist   _____ Not in Mental Health Field
_____ Clinical Social Worker   _____ Other:_____

◆   ◆   ◆

Professional Resource Press
P.O. Box 15560
Sarasota, FL 34277-1560

Telephone #941-366-7913
FAX #941-366-7971